T0037861

LUNCHBOX

Also by
Marnie Hanel and Jen Stevenson

The Picnic
The Campout Cookbook
Summer: A Cookbook
The Snowy Cabin Cookbook

LUNCHBOX

So Easy, So Delicious, So Much Fun to Eat

Marnie Hanel and Jen Stevenson

ARTISAN | NEW YORK

On the cover: Bearwich: Cinnamon Maple Sunflower Seed Butter (page 46) and Speedy Strawberry Jam (page 47) sandwich stamped into a bear shape with strawberry ears and nose, raisin eyes, and an endearingly wobbly jam smile (piped with a squeeze bottle or sandwich bag with a corner cut off) on Sprinkle Popcorn (page 122) + mixed berries + cheese cubes + Persian cucumber coins

Text and photographs copyright © 2022 by Marnie Hanel and Jen Stevenson

All rights reserved. No portion of this book may be reproduced—mechanically, electronically, or by any other means, including photocopying—without written permission of the publisher.

Library of Congress Cataloging-in-Publication Data is on file.

ISBN 978-1-64829-094-7

Design by Bonnie Siegler, 8point5.com

Artisan books are available at special discounts when purchased in bulk for premiums and sales promotions as well as for fund-raising or educational use. Special editions or book excerpts also can be created to specification. For details, contact the Special Sales Director at the address below, or send an e-mail to specialmarkets@workman.com.

For speaking engagements, contact speakersbureau@workman.com.

Published by Artisan
A division of Workman Publishing Co., Inc.
225 Varick Street
New York, NY 10014-4381
artisanbooks.com

Artisan is a registered trademark of Workman Publishing Co., Inc.

Printed in China on responsibly sourced paper

First printing, June 2022

1 3 5 7 9 10 8 6 4 2

For our favorite little lunchers

Contents

IT'S LUNCHTIME

Whether they were in the metal boxes adorned with Care Bears we carried to preschool or the brown paper sacks we smashed inside our overstuffed high school backpacks, we've enjoyed school lunches aplenty. But it wasn't until we started teaching kindergarten (Jen's former occupation) and raising three small children (Marnie's current preoccupation) that we gave much thought to who was packing the lunchbox. If you have kids, no matter your inclination or abilities, you will spend thousands of hours planning, shopping for, and preparing lunch. Given this, you have two choices: you can see lunch as relentless parent homework, or you can see it as a golden (or metal or plastic) opportunity.

You can use their lunchbox as a way to clear your fridge, foisting dinner leftovers on the daytime crowd. You can use it to clear your mind, creating an orderly Zen garden (via neatly stacked celery sticks and carrot chips) out of a chaotic produce door. You can use it to start a conversation about the school day ("What did so-and-so have for lunch?") or food combinations ("You like oranges, you like grapes—how 'bout oranges *with* grapes?") or food groups ("Can you point to your protein item? Why did you only eat your dessert?"). You can use it to tee up success for babysitters and grandparents, playdates, zoo trips, and travel of all sorts. You can use it to teach kids about shapes, colors, numbers, and holidays. You can use it to reduce single-use plastic and talk about why that's important. And, yes, you can use it to Insta-brag. (The bento-style lunchbox we explore in this book, which is inspired by the ingeniously organized and portioned Japanese

version, is primed for wow-factor—if that's your thing.)

Of its many wondrous qualities, we think the lunchbox's superpower is in transforming wiggly, capricious eaters into a captive culinary audience. Far from the kitchen and tired grown-ups primed to cave and make noodles, your kid may finally "try new food 'cause it might taste *gooooood*." (That's Daniel Tiger, for the new parents in the back.) Or they might flag down their pre-K teacher to dictate a note for home that reads, "I do not like cheese," to which you might reply, "That was not cheese. That was a yellow pepper." Or they may leave carrots in the lunchbox four times, then eat them the fifth time because they're sliced on an angle—and, also, because Myla is eating them. In any case, every time kids engage with food without an accompanying power struggle, you're winning. Whatever you do, don't sleep on the chance to benefit from other parents' victories, too. We've leaned into peer pressure to expand our lunch options to include Simone's probiotic yogurt, Genzo's onigiri, and Benjamin's burrito, which (in case you're wondering) gets tucked into a thermos to stay warm but is also accepted at room temperature.

The influence of lunchbox envy can, of course, go the other way, sending you in directions you've previously avoided, for instance, down the rabbit hole of elaborate bento boxes. Our advice on this hobby: know thyself. If you are among those whose heart sings at the sight of a sandwich shaped like a school bus, have we got a chapter for you! (It's chapter 4, "Knock Yourself Out.") If, on the flip side, you have a whimsical bent but do not want to spend more than five to ten minutes making lunch, dog-ear all the lunchboxes that involve undemanding food cutouts—or turn to chapter 2, "Bunches of Lunches," where you'll find myriad ways to pack lunchboxes that are more impressive and fun than the effort implied. Also keep an eye out for the "Cheat Sheets" in chapter 3, "Week by Week" which will guide you to shop for anything you don't want to make. (Yes, it's fine if that's everything.) If instead you bought this cookbook to, well, cook, you will also find recipes throughout the book. From everyday to extremely-special-and-I-hope-they-remember-this-always days, we've got you covered—literally, because with every lunchbox we developed, we made sure you could close the lid.

Speaking of lunchbox lids, has there ever been a better setup for dining drama? No cloche lifted at a fancy (Nancy) meal could be as suspenseful as the second your kid unhinges the lunchbox latch and opens it for the big reveal—except, perhaps, the second you lift the lid when it comes home. (Finding the lunchbox empty is a rare parenting gold star.) At its best, the lunchbox is the love note you unobtrusively pass to your child in the middle of the school day, whether by including an actual message of encouragement or just thoughtful food. Yes, that might look like just a sandwich, but that sandwich tells a kid someone cares enough to remember they like turkey and lettuce (but never mayo) and, no matter how tough the school day, that someone who took the time to cut that sandwich into a unicorn is waiting on the other side of it. Lunch might be the most unsung meal, but it can also be the most meaningful one.

We hope this book provides company in your night kitchen, acts as a vision board of all manner of edible delights, sparks inspiration, spurs conversation, invites loads of lunchbox laughs, and feeds your wild things. More than anything, though, we hope it reassures you that you're doing great. At the end of the (school) day, lunchbox success is a fait accompli—sending your kid out into the world is in itself a victory.

Now, let's do lunch!

xo,

Marnie + Jen

CHAPTER
1

LUNCH
logistics

LIVING THAT
LUNCHBOX LIFE

Your lunch-packing life begins by stocking up on a few supplies. This sounds simple but (like all things related to parenting products) can quickly become overwhelming, given the number of choices on the market combined with the fact that you've probably never before given two seconds' thought to something that now seems determinate of your child's happiness and success. Luckily, we've done a lot of thinking about lunchboxes, and we'll tell you everything (or perhaps a bit more than) you need to know. This chapter will save you from rookie errors, ho-hum lunch menus, and decision fatigue, answering questions such as: "Why do some lunchboxes have three compartments and others have six?" "Why did my kid's backpack come with this identical tiny backpack?" "What do I put in this thing?" "What can possibly fit in the tiny circle compartment?"

Herewith, we'll set you up for lunchbox laurels, answering all questions about selection criteria for supplies; introducing inspiration for snacks, sandwiches, and more; and building a curated collection of tools and flair to make lunch fun for kids to eat and grown-ups to make.

LUNCHBOX LIFTOFF

**Before you can pack, first you must prep.
Start by gathering the following essential supplies.
Yup, lunch has changed a lot since you went to school.**

LUNCH BAG

What is this?

Once upon a Generation X and Z, kids only needed a lunchbox. Now they need a lunchbox and a lunch bag. (Why?!?) Sometimes called a "lunchie" or a "lunch buddy" or a "very small and redundant but somehow essential backpack," this tiny soft cooler is designed to keep food at a safe temperature until lunchtime.

Parent Pointers

Not all lunchboxes fit in all lunch bags. (There's not a universal size, and many require a proprietary bag.) Not all bags fit in all backpacks. (Some will fill the backpack entirely.) Not all lunches will travel well in all bags. (If you're into complex bentoscapes, look for a flat-bottom bag so the box can travel in a horizontal position.) Not all children will find utensils/inspirational notes/lucky charms if stuffed inside a pocket of an insulated bag. (A zipper pocket is a black hole.)

ICE PACKS

I already have this, right?

No. You have the small, novelty-shaped, gel ice packs designed for bonks and boo-boos; and/or the thick, heavy packs for coolers; and/or a bag of frozen edamame for first aid because kids fall a lot. This is another thing. Look for slim ice packs with a hard exterior. These slip inside the insulated bag directly against the lunchbox while also allowing enough room to easily zip the bag. (Often there's a mesh interior pocket for this very purpose.) Transfer an ice pack or two from the freezer to the insulated bag to keep the lunchbox contents chilled.

Do I really need it?

Required (in some states) at daycare and optional in the years after, ice packs are useful when packing foods better eaten cold (e.g., yogurt) or prone to perishing—especially in warm climates. Some parents swear by lunchboxes with a freezable insert that fits under the food tray; others swear by freezing some of the lunchbox's contents (sandwiches, pinwheels, yogurt, fruit). We've never had great success with children accepting the ensuing texture shift, but if you do, Godspeed.

WATER BOTTLE

Can't they use a cup?
You're hilarious.

Parent Pointers
Flip-straw water bottles are easiest for young kids to open and simplest for grown-ups to refill, wash, and find. Kidding on the last one—just sending that energy into the universe for you. Your kids will forget their bottle somewhere. Write their last name on it to better the odds of its return.

HAND SANITIZER

Even at lunch?
Especially at lunch.

Parent Pointers
Spray sanitizer works for parents but can be downright dangerous in a lunchroom of bright-eyed kids with questionable aim. For the lunchbox set, look for the gel version that comes in a miniature bottle with a clip to attach to the lunch bag. (You can find these, like everything else you need for parenting, at Target.)

UTENSILS

Got 'em!
But do you want to keep 'em? Avoid slowly losing every spoon in the silverware drawer by purchasing compostable (for the forgetful) and reusable (for the less forgetful) utensils just for school. Spork, this is your time to shine. Knives are a hard no.

Parent Pointers
Look for a utensil set sold with a travel case so that dirty forks don't muss the lunch bag. Truly superior utensil sets include a ginormous rubber band or small silicone pod to attach the utensils directly to the lunchbox or bag, so kids can't miss them and insist they were left with no other option than to eat their meatballs with their hands. Which isn't saying they won't anyway.

NAPKIN

Wait. This is different, too?
Nope. Some things never change. Like that permanent splotch on your rug from spilled sensory slime.

Parent Pointers
Remember a napkin and the laundry will thank you. Forget it and there's always their sleeve.

CHOOSE YOUR OWN LUNCHBOX ADVENTURE

While it's not quite as consequential as choosing the mother/father of your children, the lunchbox you select will stick with you for many years, for better lunches or for worse, in good times and in bad, in sick days and in health, until hot lunch do you part. So it's wise to give this decision some thought, weighing the following factors.

OPENING HOURS

Lunchbox lids and latches can be tricky/impossible for kids to open. Some latches aren't intuitive for young children; some lids are difficult for tiny fingers to pry off; ~~some~~ all teachers do not want to open twenty-plus kids' lunchboxes. Together, practice opening the lunchbox at home. Or do as we once did and take your kid to a store that sells many options, present them with several, and time how long it takes them to open each. The decision might make itself.

EYES ON THE SIZE

Generally speaking, the more friendly and fanciful the lunchbox looks, the smaller its portions. These lunchboxes (which are often lighter and easier to open) are perfect for little lunchers and could last indefinitely for light eaters. For kids who want the whole sandwich (or two), you'll likely move into the larger, metal variety by second grade. If, for reasons of sustainability or preference, you start in a metal box, we recommend going for the larger size to avoid needing to repurchase and defeating the whole eco-minded point. You can always pack it at half capacity in the early years.

DIVIDE AND CONQUER

If you prefer to pack a full-sized sandwich every day, look for a lunchbox with a large enough compartment to hold one. (This usually means three compartments total, unless it's an oversized box.) If you're happy with tea sandwiches, pinwheels, and small sandwiches, and favor more food choices, you can get away with a five- or six-compartment box. Page through this book for examples of both and see what you like.

SPILL THE BEANS

Some lunchboxes have a perfect seal, so applesauce, yogurt, beans, dressed salads, and thick dips can go directly in the box. Others do not. How do you know which is which? If the company sells lidded containers as accessories, they're anticipating spillage. This doesn't mean that lunchbox is a no-go; lidded containers work great, and you can always keep things simpler by saving apt-to-spill accompaniments for dinner instead. (Tiny tip: Before school, tell young kids about the container's intended use, or else your Dilly Dip, page 58, will be reviewed as "weird yogurt.")

SET PRICE

Lunchboxes, particularly metal ones, are an investment. When you break down the price per use, though, it's a good one—and once you get one, you'll probably want two (or another removable insert) so one will be available while the other is in the dishwasher. Luckily, there are coupon and promo codes galore to make your purchase more affordable. Many lunchboxes go on sale in early summer, when only the plan-ahead types have their eye on the next school year. (Now, that's you.)

CLEAN PLATE CLUB

Unless you're a devoted by-hand washer—in which case, please come over—investigate how well the lunchbox fares in the dishwasher. Lunchboxes with removable inserts trap pesky remnants of dishwasher soap under the rim. You can use a tiny scrub brush (like the one that comes with reusable straws) to remove it, you can become a devoted by-hand washer to avoid it, or you can live with it because kids don't care. Metal lunchboxes can be washed directly in the dishwasher but, as discussed above, are often not leakproof. Some can be tough for young kids to open, and others do not fit inside a standard bag. If you're coming to the conclusion that no box is perfect, you are on the right track. It's more about deciding which flaws you can live with, since they're cute, their good traits far outweigh the bad, and, anyway, you love them. Are we still talking about lunchboxes?

LUNCHBOX LAYOUT

We photographed 100 lunchboxes for this book, but if you mixed and matched the components in every way possible, there are actually 478 factorial (indeed!) lunchboxes in these pages. (Yes, we were mathletes, thank you for asking.) In other words, once you get the hang of your kids' favorite lunch foods, there's practically no end to the lunchboxes you can make. For a five-compartment lunchbox, the essential components typically shake out as diagrammed at right. (We've included a category for the treat circle you'll see in some designs, too, since that's a fun but tricky spot. You can also swap one of the snack compartments for one of the goodies listed under Something Sweet.) Use this list for planning inspiration, possibly after reviewing it with your kid, pencil in hand.

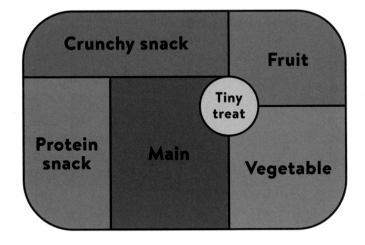

FRUIT

Apple chips	Goji berries
Applesauce	Golden raisins
Apple slices	Grapes
Apricots	Honeydew balls
Avocado cubes	Kiwi moons
Banana chips	Mango cubes
Blackberries	Olives (pitted)
Blueberries	Orange wedges
Cantaloupe balls	Pear slices
Cherries	Pineapple triangles
Cherry tomatoes	Plum slices
Dehydrated berries	Pomegranate seeds
Dried apricots	Raisins
Dried coconut	Raspberries
Dried cranberries	Starfruit slices
Dried mango	Strawberries
Dried pineapple	Tangerines (easy peel)
Fig halves	Watermelon cubes

VEGETABLE

Bell pepper strips	Jicama sticks
Broccoli florets (steamed)	Mushroom chips
Butternut squash (steamed)	Peas
Carrot chips	Pickles of all sorts
Cauliflower florets (steamed)	Radishes
Celery sticks	Rainbow carrots
Corn (salsa/salad/cob section)	Seaweed snacks
Cucumber rounds	Snow peas
Edamame	Sugar snap peas
Green beans	Sweet pepper rings
	Sweet potato cubes
	Zucchini noodles

MAIN

Avocado sandwich	Burrito
Bagel and cream cheese	Chicken (cubed, shredded, grilled, roll-ups, sandwich, pinwheel)
Bao	
Black bean bowl	

Chicken salad
Crepes (filled)
Deli salad
Dino nuggets
Dolmas
Dumplings
Egg bites
Egg salad
Falafel
French toast sticks
Frittata wedge
Grain salad
Ham (cubes, roll-ups, sandwich, pinwheel)
Hummus sandwich
Leftovers
Mini corn dogs
Mini meatballs
Mini pancakes
Mini pizza
Mini quiche
Mini waffle
Mortadella (cubes, roll-ups, sandwich, pinwheel)
Onigiri
Pasta salad

PB + J
Peanut noodles
Pork tenderloin slices
Quesadilla (stuffed with veggies)
Roast beef (roll-ups, sandwich, pinwheel)
Salami (cubes, roll-ups, sandwich, pinwheel)
Salmon (grilled, smoked)
Sausage
Skewers
Steak bites
Strawberry + brie baguette sandwich
Summer rolls
Sushi
Tabbouleh
Tea sandwiches
Tempeh tenders
Tofu
Tortellini
Turkey (cubes, roll-ups, sandwich, pinwheel)
Veggie-packed pinwheels

CRUNCHY SNACK

Beet crackers
Breadsticks
Cauliflower crisps
Cheddar bunnies
Corn chips
Crackers
Crostini
Crunchy corn
Pea crisps
Pita chips
PopChips

Popcorn
Potato chips
Pretzel crackers
Pretzels
Puffed rice chips
Rice cakes
Rice cracker mix
Tortilla chips
Trail mix
Veggie chips
Veggie straws

PROTEIN SNACK

Almonds
Ants on a log
Babybel cheese
Bamba peanut butter puffs
Beef stick or jerky
Cashews
Cheese cubes/slices/sticks
Chickpeas
Cottage cheese
Crunchy chickpeas
Feta
Hard-boiled egg
Hummus

Kind bar
Nut butter
Peanuts
Pecans
Pepitas
Pistachios
String cheese
Tempeh
Turkey bacon
Turkey sticks or jerky
Walnuts
Yogurt

SOMETHING SWEET

Almond butter cup
Animal crackers
Banana bread
Blueberry mini muffin
Brownie
Chocolate-covered pretzels
Cookies
Dark chocolate wedge
Energy bites
Fig bar

(More) fruit
Lemon mini muffin
Letter cookies
Licorice
Mini cupcake or pastry
Pocky
Protein bar, cut into strips
Pudding
Pumpkin bread
Yogurt-covered pretzels
Zucchini bread

TINY TREAT

Chocolate button candies
Chocolate chips
Fruit snacks
Good-luck charm
Gummy bears
Jelly beans
Just a few berries
Marshmallows

Chocolate nut-butter cup
Note from home
Novelty pin for backpack
Single strawberry
Tiny contraband toy
Wafer cookies
Yogurt-covered raisins
Yogurt drops

THE STANDBY SEVENTEEN

Having an actual (not mental) list of your no-fail lunch foods in your phone makes it easier to speed through the store without forgetting anything, or hand off the grocery shopping duty. This is the list that can get us through any school week, and it's where we'll start when we hand off lunch-making. Use ours, or take a photo of your kid's lunchbox for a couple of weeks and make your own.

FRUIT
- [ ] Tangerines
      (seedless, easy to peel)
- [ ] Strawberries
- [ ] Grapes

VEGETABLE
- [ ] Carrot chips
- [ ] Red bell pepper
- [ ] Cucumber

MAIN
- [ ] Sandwich bread
- [ ] Cream cheese/nut butter
- [ ] Jam
- [ ] Turkey

PROTEIN SNACK
- [ ] Hard-boiled egg
- [ ] Block of cheese
      (to cube or slice)
- [ ] Hummus

CRUNCHY SNACK
- [ ] Pretzels
- [ ] Trail mix

SOMETHING SWEET
- [ ] Small cookies
      (kids like to see *more*)
- [ ] Chocolate chips

STARTER SANDWICHES

Every little luncher has a two-ingredient (or one . . . let's not push it!) soul-mate sandwich that gets them started. If you're drawing a blank on what your kid's signature sammy could be, here are a few in heavy lunchroom rotation.

PB + J (see page 42 for more on that)
Almond butter + honey
Sunflower seed butter + apple slices
Peanut butter + banana
Cheese + tomato
Hummus + cucumber slices
Hummus + turkey
Butter + cucumber

Turkey + cheese (or not) + mustard/mayonnaise
Ham + cheese (or not) + mustard/mayonnaise
Salami + cheese (or not) + mustard
Cream cheese + ham
Cream cheese + turkey
Cream cheese + jam
Just cream cheese (gotta start somewhere)

TEACHER'S HELPER

At home, your lunch buddy has your (more or less) undivided attention; at school,
the grown-up in the room has a lot on their plate—sometimes literally,
because they're too busy opening kids' food containers to eat.
Make everyone's lunch a little lovelier by remembering the following.

OPEN SOURCE

Before sending yogurt tubes, applesauce packs, energy bars, or snack bags to school, see if your kid can open them independently. If not, open the packaging at home and transfer the goods to the lunchbox.

SAVED BY THE BELL

Lunchtime might be much earlier than you'd expect, particularly at a big school where the cafeteria is in constant rotation, so someone's gotta eat at 10:45 a.m. Consider how much time there is between the arrival bell and mealtime when packing foods, like frozen sandwiches you hope will thaw before lunch but may not. And, if allowed, pack snacks for later in the day.

AWWW, NUTS

PB + J is now A-OK at many schools, but if yours is a nut- (or other allergen-) free zone, remind yourself to follow the rules by stashing forbidden foods, like peanut butter, on high shelves and devoting one pantry shelf to lunch supplies.

CALLING FIVES

Lunchtime goes by fast. (The American Academy of Pediatrics recommends kids get at least twenty minutes to eat. That's quick, especially given how long it takes to find a seat/peer into other kids' lunchboxes/drop the fork your grown-up thoughtfully provided and get

another one, etc.) If you're noticing the lion's share of lunch coming back in the box, ask your kid if that's because they ran out of time. If the answer is yes, select foods that can be eaten quicker (i.e., sandwich, not soup; almonds, not pistachios in the shell) and troubleshoot some of the likely culprits of lunch time-wasting: chatting, going to the bathroom, meandering to/from the water fountain, forgetting their lunchbox. For kids who are just slow eaters, consider packing a protein-rich smoothie (see page 81); they might be faster sippers.

NO MESSING

Certain foods—spaghetti and meatballs, pho, ramen—are tough to keep tidy. (We happen to know three boys who eat these foods with their shirts off and go directly into the bathtub after.) Unless you have a fastidious foodie, save foods that are likely to spill or splatter for home.

HUNGER GAMES

Tummy rumbles can distract anyone from concentrating. Set up learning success by making sure your kid eats breakfast or another snack close to schooltime, brings a protein-packed lunch, and (if allowed) has a snack stashed for the afternoon.

BEAUTY IS IN THE EYE OF THE BREADHOLDER

The top of a sandwich isn't much to look at—unless it's a bear sandwich, in which case, chef's kiss! How far you wish to go when it comes to sandwich styling is entirely up to you. Enter the Sandwich-Maker's Matrix to gauge your ideal effort-to-amazement ratio. After this, there is no turning back.

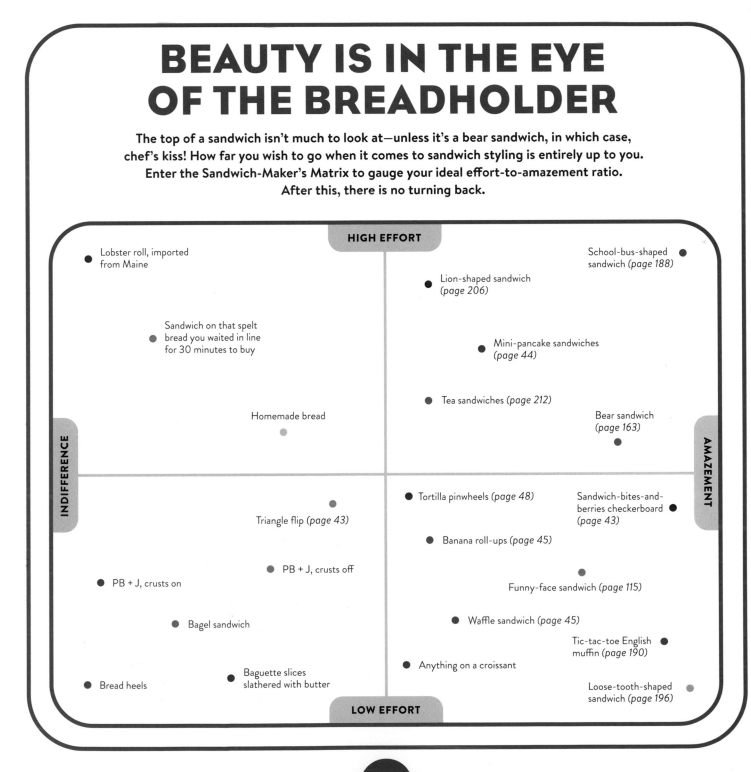

HIGH EFFORT

Lobster roll, imported from Maine

School-bus-shaped sandwich (*page 188*)

Lion-shaped sandwich (*page 206*)

Sandwich on that spelt bread you waited in line for 30 minutes to buy

Mini-pancake sandwiches (*page 44*)

Tea sandwiches (*page 212*)

Bear sandwich (*page 163*)

Homemade bread

INDIFFERENCE

AMAZEMENT

Tortilla pinwheels (*page 48*)

Sandwich-bites-and-berries checkerboard (*page 43*)

Triangle flip (*page 43*)

Banana roll-ups (*page 45*)

PB + J, crusts off

PB + J, crusts on

Funny-face sandwich (*page 115*)

Bagel sandwich

Waffle sandwich (*page 45*)

Tic-tac-toe English muffin (*page 190*)

Baguette slices slathered with butter

Anything on a croissant

Bread heels

Loose-tooth-shaped sandwich (*page 196*)

LOW EFFORT

BUILD A BETTER LUNCHBOX

If you're of a minimalist mindset, these simple styling principles require no specialty equipment.

VARIETY IS THE SPICE OF LUNCH

There's a reason there are multiple compartments in the lunchbox, and it's not to put the same thing in all of them. Showcase an array of options while observing the cardinal kid rule that unlike foods should not touch. To each—apples, celery sticks, cheese cubes, crackers, turkey roll-ups, graham cracker bears—their own.

RAINBOW BRIGHT

Pops of bright magenta raspberries, verdant sugar snap peas, golden egg yolks, or shockingly blue fruit snacks (because everyone gets to put one thing in the grocery cart) break up a ho-hum Thursday's monotone lunchbox. Pack with an eye for a full spectrum of colors for the most jaw-dropping, nutrient-rich (well, except for those blue things) lunch.

LOVE TRIANGLE

Put your knife skills to work, cutting kiwis into triangles, cucumbers into spears, mangoes into cubes, carrots into ridged chips, celery into boats, strawberries into hearts, or potatoes into a tiny replica of the Statue of Liberty (pretty sure we saw that last one on TikTok) for an impressively attractive array of fruits and veggies. Whole foods that are also visually interesting? Talk about squaring the circle.

MEASURE UP

Soon enough, you'll be a whiz lunchbox architect who intuitively cuts carrot sticks to the exact length of the compartment and knows the satisfaction of finding a store-bought granola bar just the right size for that tricky long spot at the top of the box. But while you're getting started, break out the ruler and make a mark on your cutting board (or cut a just-right-length celery stick guide) to easily cut everything to the perfect fit.

MADE TO ORDER

You may not get them to sort their 27,547-piece Lego brick collection into the (clearly labeled, so what gives?!) intricate organizational system, but you can still introduce the life-changing art of decluttering at lunchtime. Neatly stack crackers, celery sticks, and sideways sandwiches in each compartment just so, and bask in the beauty of your artful arrangement. See, you *can* have nice things.

TOOLS OF THE TRADE

**Make lunchbox magic faster than a fairy godmother
with these ingenious and affordable accessories:**

BENTO PICKS

All hail the lunchbox's most fundamental flair, which transforms it from ho-hum to hooray in less than five seconds all while offering an enticing (germ-free) alternative for wee fingers apt to pick up cheese cubes, fruit cutouts, tofu, chicken, meatballs.

CANDY EYEBALLS

Use these to add a little personality to hard-boiled eggs, sandwiches, bagels, rice cakes, sliced cheese, cookies, and all manner of fruits and vegetables. All we can say is, never has a baby carrot been met with such enthusiasm. (P.S. Need "glue"? Try honey or nut butter.)

FOOD CUTTERS

Small, sharp, assorted-shape punches are particularly well-suited for cleanly cutting cheese, fruits, vegetables, and your new countertop (hence, don't forgo the cutting board).

COOKIE CUTTERS

Custom-cut cookie dough and sandwich bread, or shape pancakes and fried eggs to match seasonal and holiday themes as well as your child's current passions (ocean life, dinosaurs, Bigfoot, you name it).

MINI ALPHABET + NUMBER CUTTERS

Here's a fun way to reinforce vocabulary words, ages, and names, or to just remotely remind your little motormouth to stop talking and E-A-T.

ONIGIRI MOLDS

Few things have a better ratio of ease-of-use to charm than rice molds. Pop in a ball of cooked rice, then pop out a fetching cat face, heart, star, fish, penguin, panda, or even fully formed Pikachu. Use nori (dried seaweed) to embellish.

SANDWICH STAMPS

From simple shape cutouts to elaborately detailed rocket ship blueprints, these clever cutters take that ubiquitous lunchbox linchpin from meh to magnificent with one swift smash.

SILICONE CUPS

These cute, colorful corrals hold extra-juicy fruits, yogurt, pudding, dips, and salads. They're also very useful for placating petite diners who prefer that their foods not touch.

WOW FACTOR 101

"Show, don't tell" is both the first piece of writing advice your kid will receive and the approach we've taken to teaching styling tricks in this book. If you're a visual learner, flipping through these photos will tell you everything you need to know. If you prefer to read the instructions, grab a pencil and keep track of your progress from lunchboxing amateur to heavyweight.

- ☐ Embellish something with candy eyeballs (p. 147).

- ☐ Transform Babybel into something even better by using a food cutter or an X-Acto knife (p. 33).

- ☐ Fan crackers, slices of hard-boiled egg, or tomato (p. 38).

- ☐ Fetchingly fold cold cuts, once lengthwise and again crosswise (p. 56).

- ☐ Snugly stack crackers to surround a dip (p. 39).

- ☐ Float a turtle (kiwi body + grape extremities) on yogurt (p. 41).

- ☐ Arrange different foods in three or more stripes like a rainbow (p. 181).

- ☐ Find an energy bar that fits perfectly into the top compartment (p. 40).

- ☐ Pack a new sassy-shaped snack, such as Trader Joe's finest dried baby pineapple (p. 41).

- ☐ Use a 1-inch food cutter to make healthful foods more tantalizing (p. 37).

- ☐ Break out the melon baller (p. 44).

- ☐ Make a sandwich with both wheat and white bread; cut into fourths and flip two segments, to create a kite pattern (p. 42).

- ☐ Nestle a sandwich in popcorn or blueberries (p. 196).

- ☐ Roll up an entire banana in a tortilla and slice (p. 45).

- ☐ Make sandwiches on mini pancakes or waffles instead of bread (p. 44).

- ☐ Cut a nut or seed butter sandwich into bites, place them side-up (so they'll stick to the box), and make a checkerboard with berries (p. 43).

- ☐ Buy a sandwich punch or large cookie cutter and decorate the shape with fruit, to silly or stunning effect (p. 206).

- ☐ Find a small whole stone fruit (plum, apricot, donut peach) that fits in the lunchbox (p. 179).

- ☐ Make the prettiest possible pinwheels (instructions on p. 48).

- ☐ Make a skewer using one, and then more, ingredients (p. 54).

- ☐ Cut deli meat into 1½-inch ribbons and practice two techniques (rolling it up and folding it accordion-style) before skewering it with cheese and veggies (p. 57).

- ☐ Pack veg standing up (p. 57).

- ☐ Toss together an impromptu trail mix (p. 56).

- ☐ Pack a lunchbox of food that's all the same color (p. 60).

- ☐ Pack a lunchbox of food that's all the same shape (p. 64).

- ☐ Pack a lunchbox of foods with names that start with your kid's first initial (p. 68).

- [ ] Pack an item that must cross the compartments to fit (p. 71).
- [ ] Cut sandwiches into fingers and pack so that the sides are facing up (p. 95).
- [ ] Nestle blueberries in raspberries (p. 71).
- [ ] Nestle veggie cutouts in veggie outlines (p. 71).
- [ ] Raid the freezer for an unexpected lunchbox item, like dinosaur nuggets (p. 70).
- [ ] Float a flower (strawberries + mint) on yogurt (p. 75).
- [ ] Roll turkey bacon into a spiral and bake it into a bite (p. 77).
- [ ] Pack a buffet of buildables, such as a taco box (p. 91) or oatmeal box (p. 77).
- [ ] Transform celery boats into edible bugs (p. 93).
- [ ] Use letter cutters to etch a message into a cookie or bar (p. 95).
- [ ] Use multiple bento forks and picks to add pizzazz (p. 131).
- [ ] Turn a hard-boiled egg into an olive-eyed owl (p. 99).
- [ ] Use letter cutters to send a message in cheese (p. 99).
- [ ] Pack olives, pistachios, chips, or crackers to brace items that may shift in flight (p. 109).
- [ ] Make a tangerine flower with a grape center and mint stem (p. 111).
- [ ] Make a dessert that sets directly in the box, like pudding or Jell-O (p. 127).
- [ ] Add pops of color to white foods (p. 129).
- [ ] Tuck vegetable cutouts into a summer roll (p. 133).
- [ ] Skewer something unexpected: tortellini, ravioli, cubes of layer cake. (Who would object? See p. 143.)
- [ ] Arrange melon cutouts in an alternating pattern (p. 145).
- [ ] Pack a thematically appropriate napkin (p. 149).
- [ ] Cultivate a salami rose (p. 149).
- [ ] Wrap prosciutto or ham around grissini breadsticks (p. 149).
- [ ] Pack a high-value treasure (pomegranate seeds, candy, a wedge of dark chocolate) in the treat circle (p. 161).
- [ ] Pack naturally vivid produce such as purple cauliflower, fuchsia dragon fruit, or yellow star fruit (p. 70).
- [ ] Cut a burrito or wrap on the diagonal (p. 183).
- [ ] Sprinkle sprinkles on something that doesn't need sprinkles (p. 129).
- [ ] Sprinkle pomegranate seeds on everything (p. 177).
- [ ] Eat something (end of a wrap, sandwich crust, outline of fruit) because it wasn't pretty enough for the lunchbox (p. 216).
- [ ] Receive compliments from kids/teachers/social media strangers on your impressive work.

CONGRATULATIONS
You are officially an overachiever!

CHAPTER

2

BUNCHES of LUNCHES

IDEAS AND MORE IDEAS

Hello, you're busy. And tired. And perhaps slightly deficient in the inspiration department. All perfectly fine, since this chapter is light on cooking and heavy on ideas to kick a perhaps otherwise monotonous midday meal up a few notches.

Find tutorials on how to frantically throw random pantry snacks into a lunchbox in under five minutes while making it look like you spent at least fifteen; ideas for simple, nutritious toddler boxes for the littlest eaters; suggestions for skewering and pinwheeling like a pro; and fun ways to reinforce educational themes like shapes, colors, and letters. Not to mention a six-box section devoted entirely to the one true lunch icon—PB + J—with a few nut butter tweaks and structural design twists to liven things up.

Take a deep dive into the freezer, that zero-degree secret weapon that has saved our bacon (literally) far too many times to count. Get instructions on how to set up a sanity-saving prep station so you aren't chopping celery and balling melon three minutes before the carpool comes (spoiler: despite the best-laid prep plans, this will still often happen). And find recipes for virtuous, vibrant smoothies in your child's favorite color. Yup, even if it's blue.

So, on your mark, get ready, prep, pack!

PREP ACADEMY

There are two kinds of people in this world: those who cut their lunchbox fruit and vegetables in the morning, and those who do it the night before while watching Netflix. Should you be the latter, we applaud you; should you be the former, we are you. But if, like us, you strive to be an upstanding produce prepper, here are a few tips.

Designate a refrigerator section for your pre-prepared produce, so you always know where it is and when a raspberry resupply is needed.

Employ an airtight container or five to hold your bounty. We like Rubbermaid's Brilliance line (because oh, that seal) and sturdy Stasher reusable silicone pouches. Or divide everything out in a series of lidded glass jars—such as the Luminarc Working Glass series or good old mason jars—or the highly handy Yumbox Chop Chop storage cube system (pictured opposite).

Wash items when you get home from the market. Your future self will be beyond delighted to skip the tedium of rinsing radishes, salad-spinning spinach leaves, and gingerly picking produce stickers off of plums when time is tight.

Before storing, ruthlessly cull rotten grapes, cherries, berries, cherry tomatoes, etc., as they'll be eager to spoil their hapless companions.

Ripen melons and pineapples on the counter before peeling, cutting, and refrigerating in an airtight container (cut melon and pineapple are best eaten within a few days).

Store cherry tomatoes at room temperature, as refrigeration saps their peerless flavor. Due to their delicate nature, these are one of the few items we cut right before serving. For mostly aesthetic reasons, it's also best to cut oxygen-wary apples and avocados as close to serving time as possible, and rub exposed edges with a lemon wedge for extra freshness.

Hardier fare like carrots, celery, cauliflower, broccoli, sugar snap peas, green beans, mini sweet peppers, and bell peppers can be washed and cut up to three days ahead of time; leafy greens roughly the same. Cucumbers are best peeled and cut no more than two days ahead, while ever-robust radishes often have at least a week in them. (Store all of the above in airtight containers with a damp paper towel on top.)

PICKY EATERS' PLAYLIST

Sometimes, no matter how hard you cajole/plead/bribe, a particularly persnickety eater simply refuses to embrace the joys of kale, cottage cheese, and anchovies (mostly kidding about that last one). If you're currently in the noodles-and-butter zone, we recommend the following tactics and switcheroos.

EASY DOES IT

Researchers say it can take ten to fifteen attempts for a kid to try a new food, so if at first you don't succeed, try, try again. (And if that doesn't work, try it with a dip—see page 58 for ideas.) Offer new foods in small portions and shake up what's in the lunchbox every day (i.e., fifteen days of peas does not a pea-lover make). Include at least one surefire win in the lunchbox. Knowing they definitely ate *something* for lunch will free you up to be more experimental with the other sections.

TABLE TALK

Start a running conversation about lunch, using descriptive words ("crunchy," "sweet," or, you know, "revolting") to talk about the foods you ate that day. Ask what their tablemates had for lunch and if they'd like to try it. Whenever kids seem interested in something on your plate, (casually!) offer a taste—unless you're a pregnant or nursing mother, in which case, get your own, kid.

ALL IN THE TIMING

In our experience, six-year-olds will try most things, four-year-olds will try nothing, and two-year-olds will eat it if it's soft, sweet, or dissolvable. The most successful food-expanding tactic we've ever tried is . . . waiting.

SWAP MEET

Often, kids' food preferences are swayed by texture more than flavor; if you say potato, they say potato chip. So if your little luncher is only giving "no" for an answer, consider making adjustments before banishing foods to Neverland. If they've had it with hard-boiled eggs, perhaps they'd like an egg bite! If they're averse to edamame, how 'bout Edamame Mint Spread (page 53)? If they don't like raw carrots, how about steamed carrots? When in doubt, swap it out.

TAKE THE WIN

If you're raising a child with a restrictive diet or sensory sensitivities, and/or who is a diagnosed picky eater (big ups to the autism community), victory can look like trying foods cut into a new shape, accepting a new texture, eating a slightly larger sandwich bite, or looking at two foods that touch. No matter what the win looks like, take it. Most importantly, don't fall into thinking your kid's limited list of approved foods reflects your parenting skills. It doesn't.

PORTIONING PRINCIPLES

Kids' appetites vary so much over the years that it's any parent's guess how much they'll eat on a given day. This toggling from growth-spurt-driven voracious hunger to complete uninterest and birdlike consumption can turn meals into an infuriating power struggle, but only if you let it. At home, you can keep meals low-key by dishing small portions on their plates and placing family-style bowls on the table. By allowing kids to help themselves to seconds (or . . . not), you help them learn to calibrate their intake to their appetite without feeling pressured or sensing a boundary to push. They also get used to seeing many foods on their plate and leaving foods they don't like there, which are important life skills.

In the lunchbox, the selection is predetermined, but you can still cue off your kid to determine portions. If the lunchbox returns from school licked clean, try sending a bit more food; if there's plenty of leftover lunch, send less. Just make sure that lunch chaperones are in step with your food introduction philosophy.

Although a "Clean Plate Club" mentality has fallen out of favor, since it can encourage overeating and discourage self-awareness, some caregivers and teachers will still coax kids to finish their entire lunch. If that's the case, pack on the conservative side and chat with your kid about whether they had enough to eat, and try to observe how hungry they are when they come home. On the other hand, if students are allowed to revisit their lunchbox in the afternoon, or if they ride the bus home and can eat while they do, or if they're always ravenous at pickup, include a potential afternoon snack. You could even double down and add another (wee) lunchbox, a.k.a. a snack box, to your collection. (Lunchbox: it's a lifestyle.)

The lunchboxes in this book are packed with an eye for "ooh la la," so they are all quite full. No one knows how much your kid eats better than you do, so please adjust portions accordingly.

IF THEY WON'T EAT THIS . . . TRY THIS!

kale ➡	cucumbers
deli meat ➡	cubed chicken
hummus ➡	sweet potato puree
peas ➡	pea crisps
raw cauliflower/broccoli ➡	steamed cauliflower/ broccoli
tomatoes ➡	salsa
wheat bread ➡	wheat crackers

FROZEN ASSETS

So much more than a seemingly bottomless repository for sticky ice cream cartons, stale bread, chicken stock fodder, and no fewer than twenty Parmesan rinds, the humble freezer can be a lunchbox-building lifeline when strategically stocked. Here are a few tasty tips for planning and building your frozen assets.

Keep your kiddo's favorite fruits on hand—in frozen form. Blend bananas and mangoes into smoothies (see page 81), fold thawed and drained blueberries and raspberries into waffle and muffin batters, and simmer strawberries into a batch of jam in a jiff (see page 47).

Pack protein-rich edamame pods or shelled edamame beans directly from the freezer (they'll thaw in time for lunch). Stir frozen peas or diced mixed vegetables into pasta (add to the cooking water two minutes before the pasta is finished, to quickly thaw). Stir leftover vegetables into fried rice or grain salads, or buy frozen grain mixes that already contain them.

Yes, making your own dumplings (or gyoza) is good family fun (see page 120). But if it's a particularly busy week, you can easily buy bags of frozen gyoza, give them a quick panfry or steam, and pop a pile into a lunchbox with a side of soy sauce for dipping.

Protein-rich and packed with healthy fresh herbs, falafel makes an excellent Middle Eastern–style staple. Fold a few into flatbread with hummus, serve them atop Tasty Tabbouleh (page 155) or alongside cups of Lemony Tahini Yogurt Dip (page 59), or use them to build a boulder-strewn trail for an intrepid pitasaurus (see page 166).

Frozen waffles aren't just a madcap morning stress reliever, they're also able to pinch-hit come noontime. Use cookie cutters to stamp them into fun shapes, and serve them with a tiny tub of maple syrup in a breakfast-for-lunch box (page 74). Substitute them for bread in a breakfast sandwich or BLT, or pair with chicken nuggets for lightning-quick chicken 'n' waffles.

Hit the appetizers section of the freezer aisle to throw a pint-size party. Mini quiches, tiny tacos, personal pizzas, spanakopita triangles, and pigs in a blanket are all winning options—bake during breakfast, cool, and pack with less effort than it takes to make a sandwich.

Stash an extra loaf of sandwich bread in the freezer for a midweek resupply. Tortillas freeze beautifully, take up precious little space, and unfreeze in minutes. They're a real lifesaver for those days when nothing but a pinwheel (page 48), quesadilla, or taco box (page 90) will do.

Thanks to a series of unfortunate morning events, it's highly possible you don't have enough time to panfry a quesadilla or roll a pinwheel. In which case, toss a few freezer-friendly taquitos in the toaster oven, cool, and transfer to the lunchbox alongside a lidded container of jarred salsa for dipping.

Freeze a few cookies when you bake them, and raid the frozen desserts section for fully cooked sweets that will thaw by lunchtime. Lemon bars, mini éclairs, and macarons never disappoint.

CHEESY ON THE EYES

As it turns out, those cute little red-wax-wrapped discs of gouda you always bypass on the way to the string cheese are actually one of the best ways to brighten and excite-n a lunchbox. If time's of the essence, use 1-inch food cutters to gently punch out simple shapes (star, heart, penguin) in the wax, then remove and discard to preview the soft white cheese beneath. Or pull the wax opener tab to kick-start crafting a ladybug with dots made from olives or black sesame seeds, a fierce fanged monster (a sharp paring knife yields teeth in two seconds), or a non-stealthy ninja (red isn't the best camo color).

Willing to break out your trusty X-Acto knife? (We love that enthusiasm!) Five to ten minutes, a few surface finger cuts, and many, many soft under-the-breath curses later, behold, the miracle of a hand-carved Babybel spider, Speedo (or tighty ~~whities~~ reddies, your pick), or hipster haircut. Finish off your creation with accessorizing eyeballs, whether the winking reusable bento picks in your collection or candy eyeballs. If using the latter (as pictured above), hold off on placing them until just before closing the lunchbox lid, as the eyeballs do eventually "bleed" due to the moisture in the box—which works out OK on monsters but is slightly unsettling on people.

Then pack away. Nobody puts Babybel in a corner, except for you because it fits great there.

THE LITTLEST LUNCHERS

Keep the littlest lunchers happy and practicing their pincer grasps with a small lunchbox filled with finger-friendly foods that fall into two choking-hazard-safe categories: the squishables (e.g., diced fruit, eggs, steamed veggies) and the dissolvables (e.g., yogurt drops, pea crisps, puffed rice cakes). Peanut puffs are also a surefire win; unless it's a nut-free zone, it's important to introduce allergens early and often. Just be sure to try them at home a few times first, so you can spend your workday working, not worrying.

(CLOCKWISE FROM TOP LEFT)

Bamba Box

Steamed peas

Raspberries

Bamba peanut butter puffs

Steamed sweet potato cubes

French Toast Feast

French toast, punched into star cutouts

Freeze-dried yogurt drops

Diced strawberries

Cubed chicken sausage

Pear Berry Bliss

Cubed pears sprinkled with cinnamon

Mini puffed rice crisps (such as Dang's mini Thai rice chips)

Halved blueberries

Grated Monterey Jack

Egg Bite Delight

Egg Bites (page 78), cut into quarters

Cubed cheddar

Smashed black beans

Cubed mango

Give Peas a Chance

Pea crisps

Cut-up egg whites

Cream cheese sandwich, punched into heart cutouts

Quartered grapes

Watermelon Whoa

Halved watermelon balls

Butternut squash, punched into shapes and steamed

O-shaped cereal + freeze-dried raspberries

Cubed avocado

SNACK ATTACK

You've got a busy day ahead and exactly not enough minutes to pack a brilliant and amazing lunchbox. You've got this. Wash, slice, and dice vegetables and fruit. Add a cup of hummus here, a cup of nut butter there. Mix crunchy snacks and nuts into an impromptu trail mix. Semi-artfully arrange a handful of crackers, and rest easy knowing your to-do list still has ninety-nine problems, but a lunchbox ain't one.

(CLOCKWISE FROM TOP LEFT)

Baguette Set

Rainier cherries

Blueberries

Baguette slices with butter

Sliced turkey

Sliced tomato

Sliced hard-boiled egg

Hummus Howdy-Do

Crunchy corn + pecans

Sliced mini sweet peppers

Kiwi half-moons + strawberry quarters

Dark chocolate candy buttons

Carrot Hummus (page 52) + crackers

Mini blueberry muffin + blueberries

Be Kind (Bar) Box

Kind bar

Pea crisps

Strawberry halves + blueberries + cantaloupe balls

Gummy bugs and butterflies

Green olives + turkey jerky cut into coins + Cheddar cubes

Persian cucumber coins + cherry tomato quarters

Nut Butter Bonanza

Rainier cherries + almonds

Gummy fruit

Rice cake crackers + nut butter

Sliced purple plum

Protein bar slivers + crunchy chickpeas

Crinkle-cut carrots + sugar snap peas

Summer Sausage Social

Pita crackers

**Dark chocolate almond butter cup
with a gummy star**

Sliced mini sweet peppers

Crunchy chickpeas

**Sliced summer sausage
+ Monterey Jack**

Tomato wedges + cornichons

Kiwi Turtle Yogurt Yowza

Crinkle-cut carrots

**Dark chocolate triangle +
dark chocolate candy buttons**

**Vanilla yogurt with a
kiwi-grape turtle on top**

**Halved cocktail cucumbers
+ tomato wedges**

Mini puffed rice crisps

Dried pineapple + cashews

PB + J ALL DAY

What would we do without that old lunchtime faithful, the humble but mighty peanut butter and jelly? Any way you slice it, this beloved classic satisfies, and since you can mix and match breads, nut and seed butters, and jams to suit every sort of dietary preference, nobody's left out of the PB + J party. See what sandwich style inspires you, and if you're in a jam- or butter-making mood, turn the page to DIY.

(CLOCKWISE FROM TOP LEFT)

Blueberry Bicolor

Pea crisps

Shelled pistachios

**Bicolor cashew butter and Speedy
Strawberry Jam (page 47) sandwich (to
make this geometric magic, use dark
wheat bread on top and white bread
on the bottom, cut the sandwich into
triangles, then flip over two opposing
triangles) + nest of blueberries**

Cantaloupe balls

Raspberry Checkerboard

**Almond butter sandwich cubes +
raspberries checkerboard**

Apricot Jam (page 47) for dipping

**Pretzel twists + dark chocolate
candy buttons**

Persian cucumber coins

Pancake Stacks

Mini-pancake (page 79) sandwiches with peanut butter and raspberry jam + cherries

Kiwi quarters

Hard-boiled egg (page 105)

Mini chicken maple breakfast sausages

Strawberry Baguette

Cantaloupe and honeydew melon balls

Pistachios

Cinnamon Maple Sunflower Seed Butter (page 46) and fresh strawberry baguette sandwich

LU Le Petit Écolier (Little Schoolboy) cookies

Sugar snap peas

Hard-boiled egg (page 105)

Strawberry Waffle

Sandwich made with waffles (page 79), Honey Vanilla Almond Butter (page 46), and fresh strawberries + more strawberries

Persian cucumber coins

Dried pineapple + confetti cookies + slivered almonds

Crinkle-cut rainbow carrots

Banana Bites

Watermelon sticks

Sheet of lavash bread spread with peanut butter and rolled around a whole banana (cut the banana in half if its curviness is disrupting your flow), then sliced into rounds

Raspberry jam for dipping

Sliced celery

You've long declared your peanut butter loyalty to Jif, Skippy, Teddie, or Justin, and we're not about to come between you. But when it comes time to try a peanut-free spread, whether for reasons of school safety or shaking things up, these recipes are kid-approved winners. If you ask us, this more than justifies the purchase of a food processor, which is the chopping/shredding/blending star of our hardworking kitchens.

HONEY VANILLA ALMOND BUTTER   MAKES ABOUT 2 CUPS

3 cups raw almonds
1 tablespoon honey
1 teaspoon pure vanilla extract
¼ teaspoon kosher salt
1 tablespoon coconut oil (optional)

1. Preheat the oven to 350°F.
2. Spread the almonds on a large rimmed sheet pan and roast until fragrant and a shade darker (don't let them burn!), 15 to 17 minutes, tossing halfway through. Let cool completely, at least 2 hours, preferably 4.
3. Transfer the almonds to a food processor and grind until smooth, 5 to 7 minutes, stopping to scrape the sides as needed. Add the honey, vanilla, and salt, and process until smooth and creamy, 7 to 9 more minutes. At this point, if you'd prefer a looser texture, add the coconut oil and process for 2 more minutes. Store in an airtight container in the refrigerator for up to 2 weeks.

CINNAMON MAPLE SUNFLOWER SEED BUTTER   MAKES ABOUT 2 CUPS

1 pound (about 3 cups) hulled
   raw sunflower seeds
1 tablespoon ground cinnamon
1 tablespoon coconut or avocado oil
2 tablespoons maple syrup
½ teaspoon kosher salt

1. Preheat the oven to 350°F.
2. Spread the sunflower seeds on a large rimmed sheet pan and roast until fragrant and lightly browned (don't let them burn!), 13 to 15 minutes, tossing halfway through. Let cool completely, at least 1 hour.
3. Grind the seeds in a food processor until smooth, about 10 minutes, stopping occasionally to break up the mixture with a spatula if necessary. Add the cinnamon, oil, maple syrup, and salt, and continue processing until smooth and creamy, 5 to 7 minutes, scraping down the sides of the bowl as needed. Store in an airtight container in the refrigerator for up to 2 weeks.

Make the most of the inevitable overage from excursions to the U-pick farm with our quicker-than-quick refrigerator jams. When we're not DIYing, we're buying Crofter's organic or Trader Joe's reduced-sugar preserves for lunchboxes; they have significantly less added sugar than most store-bought jams, and no kid's the wiser.

SPEEDY STRAWBERRY JAM   MAKES ABOUT 1½ CUPS

1 pound strawberries,
  coarsely chopped
⅔ cup sugar
1 tablespoon fresh lemon juice

1. Combine the strawberries, sugar, and lemon juice in a 3-quart saucepan. Bring to a low boil over medium-high heat, stirring often and smushing the strawberries with a spatula or wooden spoon, until thick and syrupy, with just the right amount of chunkiness (your choice), about 15 minutes.
2. Transfer the jam to two sterile 8-ounce mason jars, and store in the refrigerator for up to 2 weeks or in the freezer for up to 6 months.

APRICOT JAM   MAKES ABOUT 1½ CUPS

1 pound very ripe (mushy is fine)
  apricots, pitted and
  coarsely chopped
⅓ to ½ cup honey (to taste,
  depending on how ripe/sweet
  your apricots are)
½ teaspoon fresh lemon juice

1. Combine the apricots and honey in a 3-quart saucepan. Bring to a low boil over medium-high heat, stirring often and smushing the apricots with a spatula or wooden spoon, until thick and bubbly, with just the right amount of chunkiness (your choice), about 10 minutes. Mix in the lemon juice. Taste and add more honey if desired.
2. Push the jam through a sieve with a spatula to trap the apricot skin, if desired. Transfer the jam to two sterile 8-ounce mason jars, and store in the refrigerator for up to 2 weeks or in the freezer for up to 6 months.

ROLL CALL

Sure, pinwheels might look like child's play, but there's a certain art to the stuff-and-roll technique. Err on the side of understuffing, lest the tortilla pop, gently apply palm pressure to tuck as you roll to keep fillings condensed, set on the counter for several minutes to get settled, and use a sharp knife to slice, not mangle. When making more than one roll, choose a medley of tortillas (white, wheat, spinach, or tomato) and mix and match slices for maximum splendor.

(CLOCKWISE FROM TOP LEFT)

Classic Club

Club sandwich pinwheels (spread a plain tortilla with mayonnaise, layer with sliced turkey and ham, cooked turkey bacon, cheese, and iceberg lettuce, then roll and slice)

Halved dill pickle

Cherry tomato skewers

Veggie chips

Gummy bears

Salami Pickle

Everything-spice pretzel crisps

Apricot wedges + strawberry quarters + raspberries

Pickle roll (spread a plain tortilla with cream cheese, layer with salami, place a pickle/multiple pickles a few inches from one edge of the tortilla, then roll and slice)

Green olives + sliced celery

Gummy bugs and butterflies

Strawberry Cream Cheese

Rice, pea, and black bean crisps (Off the Eaten Path)

Persian cucumber half-moons + sugar snap peas cut diagonally

Strawberry spinach roll (spread a spinach tortilla with Strawberry Cream Cheese, page 53, layer with fresh spinach leaves, line up a row of whole hulled strawberries head-down a few inches from one edge of the tortilla, then roll, and slice right down the middle of each berry)

Watermelon (punched into heart cutouts) + raspberries

Strawberry-yogurt-covered mini pretzels

Tofu Mango

Mango tofu roll (spread a whole-wheat tortilla with Edamame Mint Spread, page 53, layer with very thin cucumber slices cut with a vegetable peeler, line up tofu batons and sliced mango a few inches from one edge of the tortilla, then roll and slice)

Sliced red bell pepper

Red and green grapes

Puffed rice roll

Almonds + goji berries

Veggie Hummus

Sliced mango with a teeny-weeny lime wedge

Cauliflower puffs + pea crisps

Rainbow roll (spread a tomato tortilla with Carrot Hummus, page 52, and layer with fresh spinach leaves; line up julienned carrots, sliced bell pepper, and avocado slices a few inches from one edge of the tortilla, then roll and slice)

Halved rainbow cherry tomatoes + Persian cucumber coins

Strawberry pâté de fruit

Turkey + Apricot Jam

Turkey apricot roll (spread a tortilla with cream cheese and Apricot Jam (page 47) layer with sliced turkey and iceberg lettuce, line up shredded carrots a few inches from one edge of the tortilla, then roll and slice)

Green apple wedges + purple plum

Mini puffed rice crisps

Tomato quarters + celery sticks

Shelled pistachios

Splendid SPREADS

Whether the glue for a wrap, the sell for a sandwich, or a sneaky smuggler of vegetables, these quicker-than-quick recipes spread the love. And they're all just a whirl away in the blender (or food processor).

HUMMUS MAKES ABOUT 2 CUPS

1 (15.5-ounce) can chickpeas
  beans, drained and
  liquid reserved

¼ cup tahini (we like Soom)

3 tablespoons fresh lemon juice

2 tablespoons extra-virgin olive oil

1 large garlic clove

1½ teaspoons ground cumin

1 teaspoon kosher salt

½ teaspoon paprika

Combine the chickpeas, tahini, lemon juice, olive oil, garlic (omit for picky eaters), cumin, salt, and paprika and ⅓ cup of the reserved chickpea liquid in a high-speed blender or food processor. Blend on high until very smooth, about 2 minutes, scraping down the sides of the bowl with a spatula as needed. Transfer to an airtight container and refrigerate for up to 5 days.

VARIATIONS: *For **Spinach Hummus**, add 2 cups lightly packed fresh spinach (about 2 ounces) before blending. For **Carrot Hummus**, slice 2 large carrots into ½-inch coins and boil until tender, about 8 minutes, then blend with the other ingredients.*

PRESTO PESTO MAKES ABOUT 1 CUP

3 cups loosely packed fresh basil
  leaves

½ cup grated Parmigiano-Reggiano

½ cup extra-virgin olive oil

3 garlic cloves, minced or grated

1 teaspoon kosher salt

½ teaspoon black pepper

½ teaspoon grated lemon zest

1 teaspoon fresh lemon juice

Combine the basil, Parmigiano-Reggiano, olive oil, garlic, salt, pepper, and lemon zest and juice in a high-speed blender or food processor and blend until smooth, about 2 minutes, scraping down the sides of the blender jar with a spatula as needed. Transfer to an airtight container and refrigerate for up to 5 days (top with a thin layer of olive oil to ward off unsightly oxidation).

EDAMAME MINT SPREAD   MAKES ABOUT 1 CUP

8 ounces shelled edamame

¼ cup mint leaves

¼ cup extra-virgin olive oil

2 tablespoons fresh lemon juice

½ teaspoon kosher salt

Combine the edamame, mint, olive oil, lemon juice, and salt in a high-speed blender or food processor. Blend on high until very smooth, about 2 minutes, scraping down the sides of the bowl with a spatula as needed. Transfer to an airtight container and refrigerate for up to 5 days.

STRAWBERRY CREAM CHEESE   MAKES ABOUT 1 CUP

8 ounces cream cheese,
  at room temperature

½ cup dehydrated strawberries

2 tablespoons honey

½ teaspoon pure vanilla extract

Combine the cream cheese, strawberries, honey, and vanilla in a high-speed blender or food processor. Blend on high until smooth but still speckled with bits of strawberry, about 1½ minutes, scraping down the sides of the bowl with a spatula as needed. Transfer to an airtight container and refrigerate for up to 5 days.

VARIATIONS: *For **Raspberry Cream Cheese**, substitute ½ cup dehydrated raspberries for the strawberries. For **Blueberry Cream Cheese**, substitute ½ cup dehydrated blueberries for the strawberries.*

A CUT ABOVE

To achieve the cleanest cut on a shaped sandwich, assemble the sandwich, refrigerate it overnight, and then use a cookie cutter to punch out your desired shape. If you're loathe to toss the outline, use food cutters to punch out tiny sandwiches (e.g., stars, hearts, clouds) to surround the shape, or serve your sandwich's "shadow" (how's that for a rebrand?) as an after-school snack.

LUNCH ON A STICK

Few things are more fun than food on a stick (think: corn dogs, Popsicles, dango, burnt marshmallows), so we took a few lunchtime favorites like fruit salad, ham and cheese, and Hawaiian pizza, and put a pin in them. Well, actually a very cute wooden skewer (accompanied by a quick and concise "do not eat this" reminder), but you get the idea. When packing for small children, substitute (unlicked) lollipop sticks for picks, or use garden shears to snip off the sharp point of a pick.

(CLOCKWISE FROM TOP LEFT)

Tutti Frutti

Cashews + vanilla almond yogurt + shortbread cookies

Fruit skewers (tangerine wedge + watermelon triangle + strawberry + cantaloupe ball; apricot half + pineapple triangle + green grape; blueberries)

Cucumber sushi rolls

Rainbow Salad

Cherries

Rainbow veggie skewers (red cherry tomatoes + accordion-folded carrot ribbon + yellow cherry tomato half + Persian cucumber chunk + trimmed sugar snap pea + small boiled purple potato half)

Dilly Dip (page 58) + butternut squash pretzels

Aperitivo Hour

Salami skewers (cantaloupe flower cutouts + salami slices folded into eighths + cherry-tomato-size mozzarella balls) + taralli crackers

Bunch of grapes

Optional cannoli from the corner bakery (you could, of course, swap in cherry tomatoes and green olives, but that'd be slightly less fun)

Say Aloha

Ham 'n' pineapple skewers (pineapple grilled over medium-high heat on a grill or in a grill pan, 4 to 5 minutes per side + slices of ham cut in half and folded twice)

Barbecue popped potato chips

DIY tropical snack mix (banana chips + macadamia nuts + goji berries + shredded coconut)

Dill with It

Ham sam skewers (ham ribbon, see page 111 for technique tutorial + pickle chunk + Colby cube) + round crackers + Honey Mustard (page 59)

Quartered radishes

One perfectly ripe and delicious summer peach

Cobbled Together

Cobb salad skewers (sliced chicken or turkey, cut into 1½-inch strips and rolled + cherry tomato half + hard-boiled egg quarter + sliced ham, cut into 1½-inch strips and rolled)

Cilantro Avocado Dip (page 58) + carrot sticks, cucumber sticks, celery sticks, and bell pepper sticks

Everything-spice pretzel crisps

TAKE A *Quick* DIP

Save your little dipper from lunchbox spillage by packing all dressings and sauces in small lidded containers unless the dip is very thick and the lunchbox is leak-free. Even then, err on the side of caution. It's better to be safe than sorry-your-cookies-are-smothered-in-honey-mustard.

DILLY DIP   MAKES ABOUT ½ CUP

½ cup plain yogurt

1 teaspoon Dijon mustard

1 tablespoon fresh lemon juice

1 small garlic clove (optional)

¼ cup chopped fresh dill

½ teaspoon kosher salt

¼ teaspoon black pepper

Combine the yogurt, mustard, lemon juice, garlic (if using), dill, salt, and pepper in a food processor and pulse until smooth. Store in an airtight container in the refrigerator for up to 3 days.

CILANTRO AVOCADO DIP   MAKES ABOUT 1½ CUPS

1 bunch fresh cilantro

1 small ripe avocado

¼ cup extra-virgin olive oil

2 tablespoons fresh lime juice

1 large garlic clove

½ teaspoon kosher salt

¼ teaspoon black pepper

Combine the cilantro, avocado, olive oil, lime juice, garlic, salt, pepper, and ¼ cup water in a food processor and puree until smooth. Store in an airtight container in the refrigerator for up to 5 days.

LEMONY TAHINI YOGURT DIP MAKES ABOUT ¾ CUP

⅓ cup plain full-fat
  Greek-style yogurt
3 tablespoons water
2 tablespoons extra-virgin olive oil
2 tablespoons tahini
¼ teaspoon grated lemon zest
1 tablespoon fresh lemon juice
1 small garlic clove, grated
¼ teaspoon kosher salt

Whisk together the yogurt, water, olive oil, tahini, lemon zest, lemon juice, garlic, and salt until smooth. Store in an airtight container in the refrigerator for up to 5 days.

HONEY MUSTARD MAKES ABOUT ¾ CUP

½ cup mayonnaise
2 tablespoons Dijon mustard
2 teaspoons honey
½ teaspoon fresh lemon juice

Whisk together the mayonnaise, mustard, honey, and lemon juice until smooth. Store in an airtight container in the refrigerator for up to 5 days.

PEANUT SAUCE MAKES ABOUT 1 CUP

½ cup creamy peanut butter
¼ cup coconut milk
2 tablespoons light soy sauce
1 tablespoon honey
1 tablespoon fresh lime juice
1 to 4 tablespoons water

1. Whisk together the peanut butter, coconut milk, soy sauce, honey, and lime juice in a small bowl.
2. Whisk in the water, 1 tablespoon at a time, until you reach a dippable consistency. (Some peanut butters and coconut milks are thicker than others.)
3. Store in an airtight container in the refrigerator for up to 1 week.

EAT THE RAINBOW

Whether you're practicing color recognition, appeasing a picky eater of the "orange foods only" persuasion, or trying to distract a fussy shopper with a green food scavenger hunt—or you just enjoy a challenge (such as finding seven edible purple items at Trader Joe's)—these captivating color-coordinated boxes cast a rosy (or red, or yellow) glow over lunchtime. (For smoothies to match, check out "Drink the Rainbow" on page 81.)

(CLOCKWISE FROM TOP LEFT)

Red Box

Strawberries

Grape tomatoes

Mini sweet peppers

Cherries + raspberry yogurt
with pomegranate seeds

Beet crackers + Babybel cheese
+ grass-fed beef sticks

Orange Box

Cheddar bunnies

Tangerine

Anna's Swedish Thins + gummy carrot

Grape tomatoes + mini sweet peppers
+ steamed butternut squash crinkles
+ tomato basil hummus

Red lentil pasta + prepared roasted
red pepper sauce

Yellow Box

Pineapple wedges and stars

Steamed corn on the cob

Banana chips

Corn chips + corn salsa

Cheese quesadilla with optional corn tortilla star flair

Green Box

Pea crisps

Green Goldfish crackers + pistachios + green jelly beans

Green apple slices

Steamed broccoli + the last of a bottle of Green Goddess dressing

Cucumber avocado sushi rolls + cucumber slices + pickled ginger

Pink Box

Ham and provolone pinwheels

Strawberry yogurt + strawberry-yogurt-covered pretzels + strawberry fruit gummies + strawberry licorice

Freeze-dried raspberries

Red radishes

Beet-pickled egg (see page 105)

Purple Box

Blueberry bagel with blueberry cream cheese

Red and purple grapes + grape gummy stars + cupcake with a liberal dusting of purple sprinkles

Blue corn chips

Purple carrot sticks and cutouts

Blackberries

SHAPE UP

No mini mathematician could resist this geometric lunchbox series, and every punster parent will thrill at the STEM-ulating opening for a lunchbox note or five. A few to get you started: "It's circle time." "Hey, this lunch is all right!" "Squaring is caring." "Can you get oval this lunch?" "You're a-cute kid." "Reach for the stars!" (We'll let you take it from here.)

(CLOCKWISE FROM TOP LEFT)

Circle Box

**Beet and sweet potato chips
with salsa + Babybel cheese**

Turkey and lettuce bagel sandwich

Tangerine wheels + blueberries

**Rainbow carrot coins +
Persian cucumber rounds**

Mini cupcake with dot sprinkles

Rectangle Box

Mango slices

Checkerboard pretzels

**LU Le Petit Écolier
(Little Schoolboy) cookie**

**Celery, rainbow carrot, and
red bell pepper slices with
green goddess dressing**

**Salami, provolone, and lettuce
sandwich fingers**

Square Box

Checkerboard cookie

Cantaloupe and honeydew cubes

Everything crackers

Turkey, Cheddar, and ham cubes

Golden Grahams cereal + yogurt

Oval Box

Pringles potato chips

Banana chips + dried apricots + pumpkin seeds

Kiwi slices

Plant-based mini corn dogs + yellow mustard

Halved cocktail cucumbers and grape tomatoes

Triangle Box

Lemon bar + tangerine segments

Watermelon, feta, and cucumber salad with fresh basil

Pineapple + kiwi

Spanakopita

Pita chips + red pepper hummus

Star Box

Sliced star fruit

Carrots + cucumbers + Colby

Pita Punchies (page 154)

Watermelon and blueberry skewers

Salami and cream cheese sandwiches, made with two star-shaped biscuit cutters in different sizes

LETTERS ENTERTAIN YOU

Whether "look, there's my letter!" is your pre- reader's favorite game
or you're just checking to see if your middle schooler is paying attention,
packing only foods that start with their first initial is F-U-N-N-Y.
Just be sure to tuck a menu into their lunch bag so they'll follow the joke.

P.S. IF YOUR DAUGHTER'S NAME IS UNA, MAYBE GO WITH YOUR LAST NAME.

(CLOCKWISE FROM TOP LEFT)

A

Apple slices

Apricot + Almonds

**Letter A and
Animal cookies**

**Triple A (Avocado, Asiago,
and Alfalfa sprouts) sandwich
with hummus on seeded bread**

Ants on a log

B

Bamba peanut butter puffs

Berry mix

Butter cookies

**Bao on Butter lettuce +
a letter B cookie**

Bell pepper slices

C

Carrot Hummus (page 52) +
Crackers

Cherries

Canelé

Cottage Cheese +
Cantaloupe Cutouts +
letter C cookie

Cauliflower + Cherry
tomatoes + Carrots

D

Dinosaur Kale Chips (page 72) +
letter D cookie

Danish (Donut also works here)

Dragon fruit cubes (choose
white variety for messy eaters)

Dinosaur nuggets +
Dilly Dip (page 58)

E

Éclair, to share + letter E cookie

Elbow Macaroni Stoplight Salad (page 72)

Edamame + Egg (hard-boiled, see page 105)

F

Fig bars + Fish crackers

Focaccia + letter F cookie

Flower-shaped bell peppers and cucumbers

Frittata (page 73) in a nest of Frisée

Fancy Figgy Fruit salad

DINOSAUR KALE CHIPS MAKES ABOUT 1½ CUPS

4 cups shredded dinosaur (a.k.a. Tuscan) kale, tough stems removed

1 tablespoon extra-virgin olive oil

2 tablespoons nutritional yeast

½ teaspoon garlic powder

½ teaspoon kosher salt

1. Position a rack in the center of the oven and preheat the oven to 300°F. Line a rimmed sheet pan with parchment paper.

2. With clean hands (yours or your pint-size sous's), mix the kale and oil in a large bowl until every leaf is shiny. Stir together the nutritional yeast, garlic powder, and salt in a small bowl. Sprinkle over the kale, toss, and transfer to the prepared sheet pan. Bake for 25 minutes, using a spatula to turn once, until crisp. Let cool before transferring to the lunchbox. Best eaten within a day.

ELBOW MACARONI STOPLIGHT SALAD MAKES ABOUT 4 CUPS

2 cups elbow macaroni (use Banza chickpea noodles to add extra protein)

½ cup small broccoli florets

1 cup finely diced yellow bell peppers

1 cup halved cherry tomatoes

Dressing

½ cup mayonnaise, preferably Best Foods or Hellmann's

¼ cup buttermilk

¼ cup finely chopped fresh basil

2 teaspoons Dijon mustard

2 teaspoons sherry vinegar

2 teaspoons sugar

1 teaspoon kosher salt

½ teaspoon black pepper

1. Cook the macaroni in a large pot of salted water for 1 minute shy of the package directions. Add the broccoli and cook for a final minute. Drain and rinse with cool water. Transfer the pasta and broccoli to a large bowl along with the yellow bell peppers and cherry tomatoes.

2. To make the dressing: Combine the mayonnaise, buttermilk, basil, mustard, vinegar, sugar, salt, and black pepper in a medium bowl and whisk until smooth. (If your luncher is sensitive to specks of green, instead combine all the ingredients in a blender and whiz to obliterate them.) Drizzle over the cooked pasta and vegetables and stir to coat. Cover and refrigerate for up to 2 days. Pack in the lunchbox along with an ice pack.

GREEN PEAS AND HAM FRITTATA MAKES ABOUT 8 SERVINGS

1 tablespoon extra-virgin olive oil

1 small white onion, diced

1 garlic clove, minced or grated

½ cup peas (frozen is fine)

½ cup shredded zucchini

½ cup tiny broccoli florets

½ cup lightly packed chopped fresh spinach

½ pound ham, cut into ¼-inch cubes

8 large eggs

2 tablespoons whole milk (or heavy cream, or yogurt)

¼ teaspoon kosher salt

⅛ teaspoon black pepper

½ cup shredded Monterey Jack

¼ cup crumbled feta

Feel free to substitute any vegetables your kids prefer, such as shredded carrots for the broccoli.

1. Preheat the oven to 350°F.
2. Heat the oil in a 10-inch ovenproof skillet over medium heat. Cook the onion until soft and translucent, about 7 minutes. Add the garlic and sauté until fragrant, about 30 seconds. Add the peas, zucchini, and broccoli and cook until soft, about 5 minutes. Stir in the spinach and cook until soft, 2 to 3 minutes, then stir in the ham.
3. Meanwhile, whisk together the eggs, milk, salt, and pepper in a medium bowl. Stir in the shredded Monterey Jack. Smooth the skillet mixture until reasonably even, pour the egg-cheese mixture over the top, and let cook on the stovetop for 1 minute. Sprinkle the feta over the top, transfer the skillet to the oven, and bake until the top of the frittata is set and only jiggles slightly when you rattle the pan, 10 to 12 minutes.
4. Remove from the oven, let cool, then cut into wedges and pack in a lunchbox, or store in an airtight container in the refrigerator for up to 2 days. (Gently rewarm in a microwave or toaster oven for a few minutes if eating at home.)

HOT TIP

If your hot lunch is cold by the time it hits the table, make like a happy camper and put some pep in your prep. Pour boiling water into an insulated thermos or bowl, let sit for 10 minutes, empty the container, transfer the food into it, screw on the cap, and you're set. You probably don't need a book to tell you that you can microwave leftovers, put them in a thermos, and send your kid out the door, but if you do, see above.

BREAKFAST FOR LUNCH

Introduce kiddos to the joys of brunch early on with these Sunday-morning-worthy spreads, from a New York–style lox and bagel and trio of crepes stuffed with Nutella (or a slightly healthier nut butter, your call) to good old-fashioned oatmeal with all the fixings. Make, serve, and wait fifteen years for them to call you from a seemingly endless brunch line, at last properly appreciative of their idyllic no-reservations-required childhood repasts.

(CLOCKWISE FROM TOP LEFT)

Bagel Stop

Bagel with cream cheese and lox

Black-and-white cookie +
strawberries

Hard-boiled egg (page 105)

Capers, for sprinkling + cornichon

Sliced tomatoes + cucumbers

Crêperie Glee

Crepes (page 78) filled with Nutella,
Orange Curd (page 79), or lemon,
butter, and sugar + strawberries

Citrus rounds with fresh mint

Almond yogurt + strawberry
and fresh mint flower

Speedy Strawberry Jam (page 47)

Ready or Not
Pain au Chocolat

Pecans + coconut chips + raisins

Mini chicken maple breakfast sausages

Mini quiches

Mixed berries + melon cutouts + raspberry yogurt

Mini chocolate croissant

Galette Fête

Bakery-bought strawberry galette or hand pie

Egg Bites (page 78)

Blueberry yogurt + strawberries

Pecans

Turkey bacon + blueberries + cantaloupe cutouts

Waffle-y Good Morning

Heart-shaped waffles (page 77) + hulled strawberries cut in half to vaguely resemble hearts

Egg Bites (page 78) with red pepper cutouts + turkey bacon roll-ups

Blueberries

Oatmeal Bar Bash

Oatmeal

Mixed berries

Maple cookies

Assorted toppings—coconut chips, pecans, raisins, brown sugar

NOTE: The OmieBox (pictured here) includes an embedded thermos. Unless you own this laudable lunch innovation, pack the toppings in the lunchbox with the oatmeal in a thermos on the side.

BELL PEPPER AND SPINACH EGG BITES MAKES 12

6 large eggs

½ cup cottage cheese

1½ ounces shredded Cheddar or Monterey Jack (about ½ cup lightly packed)

½ teaspoon kosher salt

⅛ teaspoon black pepper

¾ cup diced bell pepper

¾ cup chopped steamed spinach (about 5 ounces raw), gently pressed dry

1. Preheat the oven to 350°F. Grease a 12-cup muffin pan.
2. Combine the eggs, cottage cheese, shredded cheese, salt, and black pepper in a high-speed blender and process until smooth. Distribute the bell pepper and spinach evenly among the 12 muffin cups, then pour the batter over, evenly distributing it among the cups. Bake until the tops are set and the bites are baked through, 18 to 20 minutes. (Alternatively, bake the bites in a Dash Egg Bite Maker, which does all the work for you, except the batter-making part; you still have to do that.)
3. Let cool slightly, remove from the pan, and serve immediately, or store in an airtight container in the refrigerator for up to 2 days. (Rewarm gently in a microwave or toaster oven for a few minutes if eating at home.)

LES CRÊPES MAKES ABOUT TWELVE 8-INCH CREPES

1¼ cups whole milk

4 tablespoons (½ stick) unsalted butter, melted and slightly cooled, plus more for the pan

2 large eggs

1 teaspoon pure vanilla extract

1 cup all-purpose flour

1 tablespoon sugar

Pinch of kosher salt

Pinch of ground cinnamon (optional)

Pinch of ground nutmeg (optional)

1. Combine the milk, melted butter, eggs, vanilla, flour, sugar, salt, and spices (if using) in the bowl of a high-speed blender. Blend until very smooth, 10 to 15 seconds. Cover and refrigerate for 1 hour (give it a good swirl before cooking, in case of separation).
2. Heat a 10-inch nonstick skillet over medium heat until hot and then grease it with butter. Add a scant ¼ cup of batter and quickly swirl the pan; you're aiming for a round and thin crepe. Cook until golden spots appear on the bottom, about 30 seconds, then flip and cook until set and golden-spotted on the other side, 30 to 45 seconds. Transfer the crepe to a plate, re-butter the pan, and keep going until all the batter is gone. (If the crepes stick together when you pile them, use parchment paper between them.)
3. Fill the crepes with your topping of choice (may we suggest Nutella?), and tuck into a lunchbox. Or transfer to an airtight container and store in the refrigerator for up to 3 days or the freezer for up to 1 month (if refrigerating or freezing, separate the crepes with parchment paper; thoroughly thaw before trying to pry them apart).

MINI PANCAKES AND WAFFLES   MAKES ABOUT 60 MINI PANCAKES AND TWELVE 4-INCH WAFFLES

1 cup all-purpose or
  whole wheat flour

2 tablespoons sugar

1 teaspoon baking powder

½ teaspoon baking soda

½ teaspoon kosher salt

1 cup buttermilk

1 large egg

2 tablespoons unsalted butter,
  melted, plus more to grease
  the pan

1. Whisk together the flour, sugar, baking powder, baking soda, and salt in a medium bowl. Whisk together the buttermilk, egg, and melted butter in a small bowl. Add the wet ingredients to the dry ingredients and whisk until smooth.

2. *For mini pancakes:* Heat a large skillet over medium heat until hot, grease with butter, and add batter by the teaspoonful, keeping enough space between the pancakes that you're able to turn them (we use a spatula and a skewer to flip). Cook until golden brown on the bottom, then flip and cook until golden brown on the other side. Repeat until all the batter is gone, piling the pancakes onto a plate as you go.
For waffles: Cook according to your waffle maker's directions, piling the waffles on a plate as you go.

3. Serve immediately or let cool and pack in a lunchbox. Store in an airtight container in the refrigerator for up to 2 days (up to 3 days for waffles) or in the freezer for up to 1 month. Warm in a skillet, toaster, or microwave before serving (waffles do best in the toaster).

ORANGE CURD   MAKES ABOUT 2 CUPS

1 tablespoon grated orange zest

½ cup fresh orange juice

½ cup sugar

2 tablespoons fresh lemon juice

2 tablespoons fresh lime juice

Pinch of kosher salt

6 large egg yolks

½ cup (1 stick) unsalted butter,
  cut into cubes

1. Set a fine-mesh sieve over a medium bowl and a spatula next to it.

2. Whisk together the orange zest and juice, sugar, lemon and lime juices, salt, and egg yolks in a small saucepan over medium heat. Whisk in the butter a few cubes at a time and cook, whisking continuously (don't let the curd boil), until the curd is thick enough to coat the back of a spoon (about the consistency of loose sour cream) and registers 160°F on an instant-read thermometer, 5 to 7 minutes.

3. Remove the curd from the heat and pour it slowly through the sieve into the bowl, carefully stirring and scraping with the spatula, to trap the zest and any eggy little lumps. Store in an airtight container in the refrigerator for up to 3 days (fresher is better, flavorwise).

SMOOTHIE MOVE

We eat with our eyes, and we can drink with them too (just to clarify, not literally). These six brightly hued fruit-and-vegetable-stuffed smoothies will motivate even the most skeptical of solid-food eaters to sip and slurp their daily nutrients (results hopeful but not guaranteed). Here are a few tips for better blending.

We like the extra-silky texture of an ice-less smoothie, so every recipe contains at least one frozen fruit. Keep a variety in your freezer, and if anything in the fruit bowl is looking overripe, peel it, cut it up, and add it to the collection. If all you have on hand is fresh produce, either cut it into very small pieces and freeze on a cookie sheet for thirty minutes before pureeing, or go ahead and toss in a handful of ice.

For a touch of extra protein/healthy fats/fiber, add a spoonful of nut or seed butter, coconut oil/milk, powdered greens, flaxseeds, hemp seeds, and/or chia seeds (it's far better to serve chia seeds pulverized than whole, lest you be accused of dishing up frog eggs).

Most of these recipes call for a water base to get things whirring, but you can substitute milk, nut milk, coconut milk, pea milk, soy milk, yogurt, kefir, coconut water, fruit juice, or the tail end of your morning cup of chamomile.

Want a thicker smoothie? Add more frozen fruit (particularly banana, the smoothest of smoothie smoothers). Want a thinner smoothie (or having trouble with the mixture seizing up)? Add a splash more liquid until the consistency is Goldilocks-style—just right.

Smoothies travel well when packed properly. Pour the mixture into an insulated reusable water bottle (we like Hydro Flask's 12-ounce Kids Wide Mouth or the Yeti Rambler Jr.), leaving a little headroom so little sippers can give everything a good shake before drinking. Practice doing this at home, in the proper order of operations: shake first, *then* unscrew the lid. Make double sure the lid is screwed on correctly—messy smoothie leaks are a real lunchtime buzzkill.

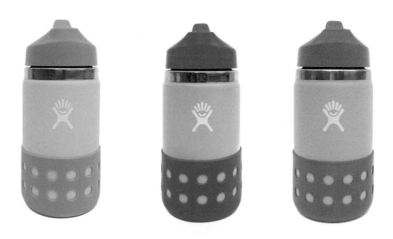

DRINK THE RAINBOW

(NO, REALLY, THESE ARE IN RAINBOW ORDER)

Directions: Combine all ingredients in order in a high-speed blender and puree until very smooth. Pack in a thermos to keep cool until lunch. Each recipe makes about 2 cups.

DRAGON BREATH

¼ cup water
2 tablespoons coconut milk
1 tablespoon fresh lime juice
½ cup cubed mango
½ cup cauliflower florets
1 cup frozen cubed red dragon fruit

BANANABERRY SPLIT

2 cups chopped strawberries
½ cup frozen cauliflower florets
½ frozen banana
¼ cup plain yogurt

Share with a friend (that's where the "split" part comes in)

POLLY PEARROT

½ cup almond milk
2 tablespoons almond butter
1 medium ripe pear, chopped (about 1 cup)
½ cup chopped carrots
½ cup frozen sweet potato cubes
½ teaspoon ground cinnamon
⅛ teaspoon ground nutmeg

ORANGE YOU DELICIOUS

¼ cup water
1 large orange, peeled and cut into chunks
½ orange bell pepper, chopped
½ cup chopped carrots
½ cup frozen cubed mango
½-inch piece peeled ginger, coarsely chopped

GREEN MACHINE

¼ cup water
1 small green apple, chopped (about ½ cup)
½ cup chopped cucumber
1 cup fresh spinach or baby kale leaves
Small handful of fresh parsley (optional)
1 cup frozen pineapple chunks

BLUEPEAR REEL

½ cup water
¼ cup chopped cucumber
¼ cup chopped broccoli florets
½ cup chopped ripe pear
1 cup frozen wild blueberries

CHAPTER

3

WEEK *by* WEEK

MONDAY TO FRIDAY LUNCH MENUS

Anyone can make one lunchbox (here's looking at you, PB + J), but making five varied, delicious, and well-reviewed lunches, week after week, month after month, for all 180 days of the school year, is a Herculean parenting challenge that requires creativity, an acute understanding of perishability, and excellent executive function, which you may or may not have after years of interrupted sleep.

This chapter allows you to go straight to the fun part without first wading through the list-making and planning. The menus are designed to maximize your groceries through reasonable repetition and remixing. Not all weeks are created equal, though, so make sure to read through the whole week's menu to determine how much you want to cook that week. We've also included cheat sheets that list store-bought substitutions when you don't want to cook at all. Shop the list on Saturday, prep on Sunday, and cook a little bit (but mostly just pack) during the week. And, if you're feeling like you want a (little) hand in the kitchen, check out the optional after-school "Group Projects" to find a recipe your kids will love to make with you. (Spoiler: It's usually cookies.)

As always, make these lunchboxes your own. Break up the menus (if you only want to make Wednesday, go for it), consult the Picky Eaters' Playlist (page 30) for worthy substitutes for any no-go fruit or veg, and feel free to simplify the styling or give it your all. (We can't help ourselves.) You certainly don't have to make the weeks in this order, but we hope each week will inspire a new way to think about how to get lunch out the door.

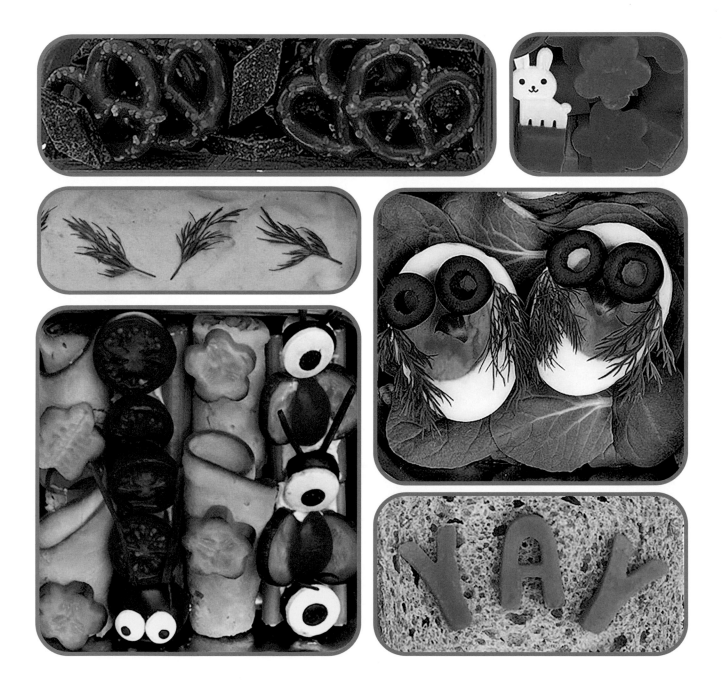

PLAY TO WIN

Kids find repetition comforting, but if you follow their lead, the menu (and presentation) can get pretty specific, pretty quickly. Same gets old fast when the feedback from the table is that the grapes and pretzels are touching, and also you cut the sandwich in four squares when it should be in two triangles.

You can encourage kids to try new foods (and enjoy it) by presenting their beloved ingredients in—sometimes slightly, sometimes drastically—different ways. (Play "Search and Find" with the cheese, chicken, turkey, olives, cucumbers, and chocolate chips in these lunchboxes to see how we shake things up in not-too-challenging, even tempting, ways.)

By merrily remixing a few staples from the family grocery list into a crowd-pleasing week of varied lunchboxes, kids will get used to all the wonderful ways their favorite foods can be enjoyed instead of just one they then come to expect. Meanwhile, the Iron Chef in your very own kitchen stadium will get some new ideas on how ingredients can overlap without directly repeating, which is helpful for both budgeting and reducing food waste.

This week's menu is built around the kid-food basics we always have on hand, and we hope it will open the (refrigerator) door to many lunchbox variations using whatever ingredients are typically in yours.

DAY 1	DAY 2	DAY 3	DAY 4	DAY 5
Taco Time	Bug-Out Box	Chicken Salad Shindig	Pinwheel Party	Fri-yay Hoot-enanny

MEAL PREP

SUNDAY

Make **Perfectly Poached Chicken** (page 88) and shred.

Use ½ cup of the shredded chicken to make **Not-So-Spicy Chicken Taco Filling** (page 88).

Use ½ cup shredded chicken to make a **Dilly Good Chicken Salad Sandwich** (page 89).

Hard-boil an egg (see page 105).

Bake a batch of **Quick Chocolate Chip Almond Flour Cookies** (page 89), or save for Monday's after-school activity if they'll never make it to Tuesday if you bake them now.

MONDAY

Raid the produce drawer and make veggie bugs.

TUESDAY

Make a chicken salad sandwich.

WEDNESDAY

Prepare your **Turkey and Dill Pinwheels** (page 88).

THURSDAY

Go owl-in for a Fri-yay surprise. "Yay!" (punched out of cheese and glued to the sandwich with honey) optional but highly encouraged.

GROUP PROJECT: Veggie bugs are a winning afternoon activity that can double as a snack. If you're in the baking mood, our one-bowl cookies are a winner, and because the recipe is egg-free, it's perfectly safe to lick the spoon while discussing the veracity of school bus stories, including, but not limited to, what comes out of your ears if you hang upside down on the monkey bars on Halloween.

SHOPPING LIST

MEAT + DELI
- [ ] 1 boneless, skinless chicken breast
- [ ] ¼ pound sliced turkey

DAIRY CASE
- [ ] 8-ounce block of Cheddar
- [ ] Greek yogurt (you'll need 1 tablespoon)
- [ ] Eggs (you'll need 1)
- [ ] Cream cheese (you'll need 1 generous spoonful)
- [ ] Hummus (or homemade, page 52)

PRODUCE
- [ ] 1 pint cherry tomatoes
- [ ] 1 pound Persian cucumbers
- [ ] 1 bag cleaned lettuce
- [ ] 1 bunch celery

- [ ] 1 lemon
- [ ] 1 pint strawberries
- [ ] 1 kiwi
- [ ] 1 bunch fresh dill
- [ ] 1 bunch fresh chives (for veggie bug antennae; optional)

BREAD + SNACK FOODS
- [ ] 5-inch tortillas
- [ ] 1 box pita crackers
- [ ] 1 loaf sandwich bread
- [ ] 1 bag pretzels
- [ ] 1 package fig cookies
- [ ] Unsweetened applesauce

PANTRY + BULK
- [ ] 1 can black olives
- [ ] 1 (15.5-ounce) can chickpeas
- [ ] 1¼ cups almond flour

- [ ] ½ cup unsweetened shredded coconut
- [ ] 1 (10-ounce) bag semisweet chocolate chunks or chips
- [ ] Extra-virgin olive oil
- [ ] Coconut oil
- [ ] Chili powder
- [ ] Paprika
- [ ] Ground cumin
- [ ] Garlic powder
- [ ] Onion powder
- [ ] Kosher salt
- [ ] Baking powder
- [ ] Pure vanilla extract
- [ ] Dark brown sugar
- [ ] Turbinado sugar
- [ ] Tahini

PRO-TIP
Take a photo of this page on your phone!

EXTRA
- [ ] Candy eyeballs (we like Wilton)

CHEAT SHEET: Looking for a shortcut? Substitute rotisserie chicken (mix with taco seasoning for Monday and mayonnaise for Wednesday), premade hummus, and a package of cookies for the recipes that follow. Make sure you update your shopping list if you choose to swap a store-bought ingredient for a homemade item.

PERFECTLY POACHED CHICKEN   MAKES ABOUT 1 CUP, SHREDDED

1 boneless, skinless chicken breast

2 teaspoons kosher salt

1 quart very cold water

Combine the chicken, salt, and water (to cover) in a medium saucepan over medium heat. When the water begins to gently simmer, reduce the heat to low, flip the chicken with tongs, and simmer for an additional 15 minutes. When the chicken reaches 165°F on an instant-read thermometer, transfer it to a cutting board to rest for 5 minutes, or until the chicken is cool enough to handle. Slice the chicken or shred with two forks, and cool completely. Pack in a lunchbox, or transfer to an airtight container and store in the refrigerator for up to 1 week.

NOT-SO-SPICY CHICKEN TACO FILLING   MAKES ½ CUP CHICKEN (FOR 1 LUNCH) AND 5 TEASPOONS SEASONING (FOR 5 LUNCHES)

2 teaspoons chili powder

1 teaspoon paprika

1 teaspoon ground cumin

½ teaspoon kosher salt

¼ teaspoon garlic powder

¼ teaspoon onion powder

½ cup Perfectly Poached Chicken (above), shredded

1 teaspoon extra-virgin olive oil

1. Combine the chili powder, paprika, cumin, salt, garlic powder, and onion powder in a small airtight container and shake to mix.
2. In a medium bowl, drizzle the chicken with olive oil, sprinkle with 1 teaspoon seasoning, and toss until fully combined. Store the remaining seasoning at room temperature in the airtight container.
3. The taco filling can be stored in the refrigerator for up to 3 days; or, if packing for the next day, scoop the chicken directly into the lunchbox and refrigerate until it's off to school.

TURKEY AND DILL PINWHEELS ON A PICK   MAKES AS MANY AS YOU WISH

1 or 2 tortillas

Cream cheese

1 fresh dill sprig, chopped

Lettuce (1 or 2 leaves)

1 or 2 turkey slices (or handful of Perfectly Poached Chicken; opposite)

Spread the tortilla(s) with cream cheese and sprinkle with dill. Add lettuce and turkey to two-thirds of the tortilla, to avoid spillage. Roll tightly, applying palm pressure, and let rest for 5 minutes. Slice into bite-size segments, and thread on a reusable pick (as pictured on page 97) or nestle together in the lunchbox.

QUICK CHOCOLATE CHIP ALMOND FLOUR COOKIES MAKES ABOUT 18 COOKIES

1¼ cups almond flour

½ cup unsweetened shredded coconut

¼ cup packed dark brown sugar

⅓ cup semisweet chocolate chunks, roughly chopped

½ teaspoon kosher salt

½ teaspoon baking powder

¼ cup applesauce

¼ cup melted coconut oil

1 teaspoon pure vanilla extract

Turbinado sugar

1. Line 2 sheet pans with parchment paper. Position 2 oven racks in the top and bottom thirds of the oven. Preheat the oven to 350°F.
2. Stir together the almond flour, coconut, brown sugar, chocolate, salt, and baking powder in a large bowl. Add the applesauce, coconut oil, and vanilla and mix until combined.
3. Using a 1½-inch spring-loaded ice cream scoop (or just a spoon or a preschooler's hand), scoop cookie dough onto the prepared sheet pans, spacing at least 1 inch apart. Gently press down each cookie to flatten and sprinkle with turbinado sugar. Bake for 12 to 14 minutes until golden. Cool completely. Pack in a lunchbox or store in an airtight container for up to 5 days.

DILLY GOOD CHICKEN SALAD SANDWICH MAKES 1 SANDWICH

½ cup shredded Perfectly Poached Chicken (opposite), chopped

1 tablespoon plain Greek yogurt

1 tablespoon finely chopped celery

1 teaspoon fresh lemon juice

½ teaspoon chopped fresh dill

Pinch of kosher salt

2 slices sandwich bread

Mix the chicken, yogurt, celery, lemon juice, dill, and salt in a mixing bowl. Spread the chicken salad evenly on one slice of sandwich bread and top with the second slice. Trim the crusts, if desired, slice, and transfer to a lunchbox. Present the sandwich sides-up for a fancy effect.

TACO TIME

**Keep a case of the Mondays at bay
with this build-your-own taco soiree.**

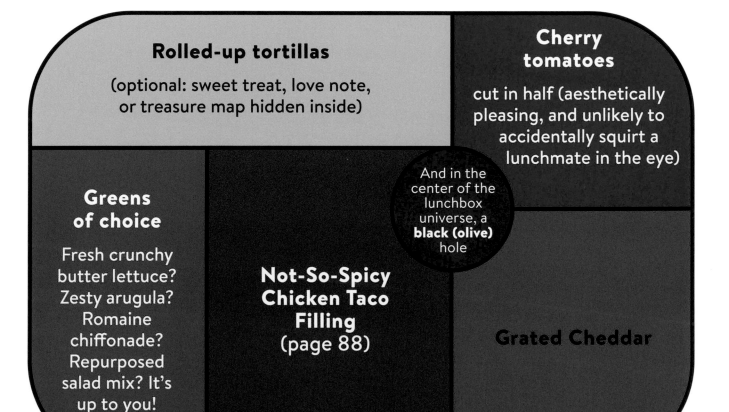

Rolled-up tortillas

(optional: sweet treat, love note,
or treasure map hidden inside)

Cherry tomatoes

cut in half (aesthetically
pleasing, and unlikely to
accidentally squirt a
lunchmate in the eye)

And in the
center of the
lunchbox
universe, a
black (olive)
hole

Greens of choice

Fresh crunchy
butter lettuce?
Zesty arugula?
Romaine
chiffonade?
Repurposed
salad mix? It's
up to you!

Not-So-Spicy Chicken Taco Filling
(page 88)

Grated Cheddar

BUG-OUT BOX

Ah! Here's that creative outlet you were looking for. (Plus, a cookie recipe to reach for any time you're tapped for snack duty.)

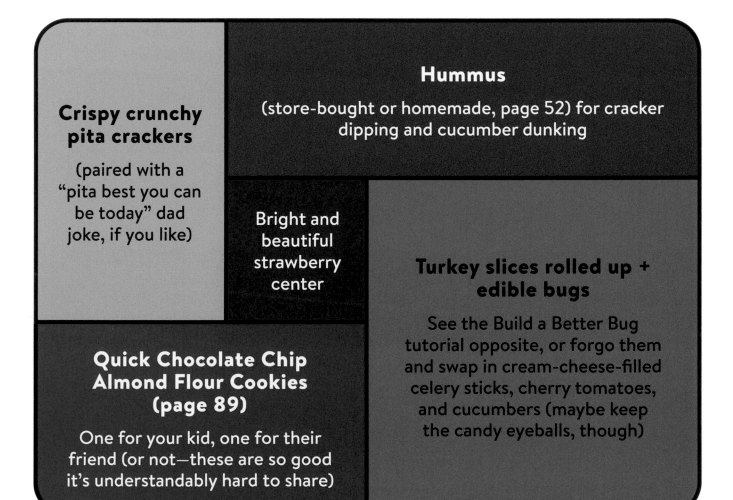

Crispy crunchy pita crackers

(paired with a "pita best you can be today" dad joke, if you like)

Hummus

(store-bought or homemade, page 52) for cracker dipping and cucumber dunking

Bright and beautiful strawberry center

Turkey slices rolled up + edible bugs

See the Build a Better Bug tutorial opposite, or forgo them and swap in cream-cheese-filled celery sticks, cherry tomatoes, and cucumbers (maybe keep the candy eyeballs, though)

Quick Chocolate Chip Almond Flour Cookies (page 89)

One for your kid, one for their friend (or not—these are so good it's understandably hard to share)

BUILD A BETTER BUG

Little did you realize your shopping list contained myriad ways to up the ants-on-a-log ante. Fill celery sticks with cream cheese or nut butter, chill in the fridge while you gather supplies, and have at it:

PRODUCE	→	POTENTIAL
Cucumber slices, strawberries, pretzels	→	Wings
Olives, grapes	→	Head
Candy eyeballs	→	Irresistible eyes
Raisins, olive bits, pimentos	→	Perfectly fine eyes
Blueberries, cherry tomatoes, olives, cereal	→	Body segments
Sesame seeds, sunflower seeds	→	Markings
Chives	→	Antennae

CHICKEN SALAD SHINDIG

Give that shredded chicken a midweek glow up.

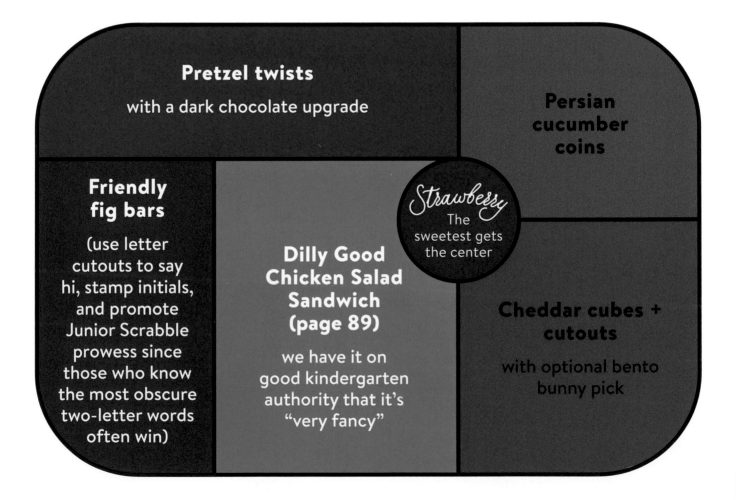

Pretzel twists

with a dark chocolate upgrade

Persian cucumber coins

Friendly fig bars

(use letter cutouts to say hi, stamp initials, and promote Junior Scrabble prowess since those who know the most obscure two-letter words often win)

Dilly Good Chicken Salad Sandwich (page 89)

we have it on good kindergarten authority that it's "very fancy"

Strawberry
The sweetest gets the center

Cheddar cubes + cutouts

with optional bento bunny pick

PINWHEEL PARTY

**Spin it, pin it, done. If your pinwheeling skills
are a bit rusty or nonexistent, see page 48.**

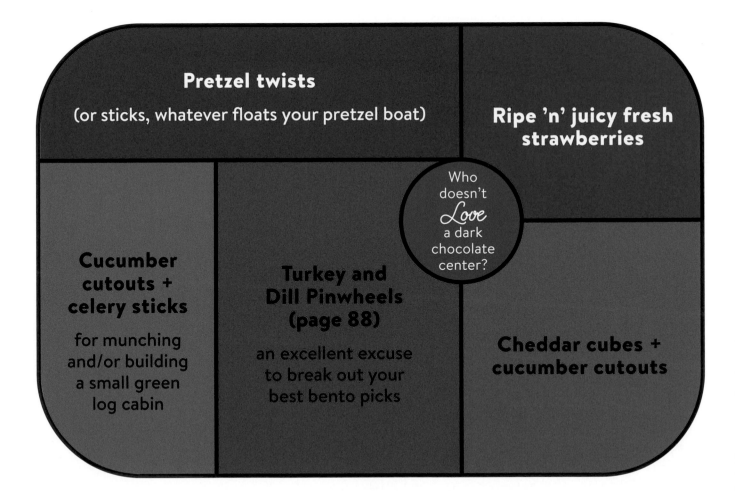

Pretzel twists

(or sticks, whatever floats your pretzel boat)

**Ripe 'n' juicy fresh
strawberries**

Who
doesn't
Love
a dark
chocolate
center?

**Cucumber
cutouts +
celery sticks**

for munching
and/or building
a small green
log cabin

**Turkey and
Dill Pinwheels
(page 88)**

an excellent excuse
to break out your
best bento picks

**Cheddar cubes +
cucumber cutouts**

FRI-YAY HOOT-ENANNY

Owl-in for the weekend.

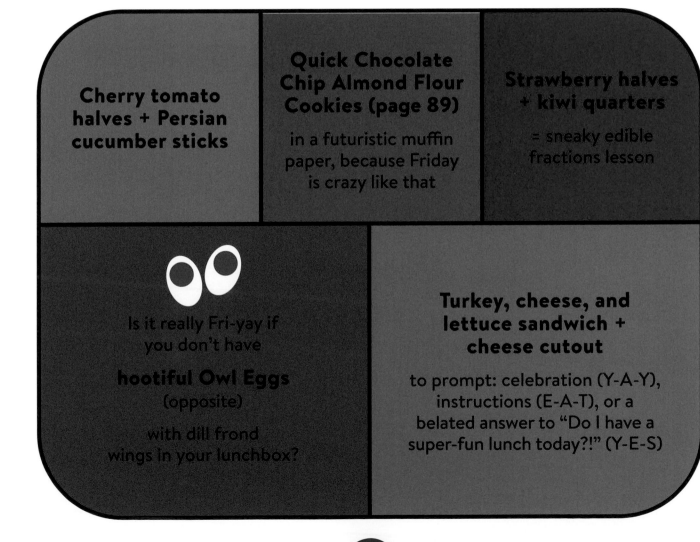

Cherry tomato halves + Persian cucumber sticks

Quick Chocolate Chip Almond Flour Cookies (page 89)

in a futuristic muffin paper, because Friday is crazy like that

Strawberry halves + kiwi quarters

= sneaky edible fractions lesson

Is it really Fri-yay if you don't have

hootiful Owl Eggs (opposite)

with dill frond wings in your lunchbox?

Turkey, cheese, and lettuce sandwich + cheese cutout

to prompt: celebration (Y-A-Y), instructions (E-A-T), or a belated answer to "Do I have a super-fun lunch today?!" (Y-E-S)

OWL EGGS MAKES 1 SERVING

1 hard-boiled egg (see page 105)
Lettuce
4 olive slices
2 tiny strawberry triangles
4 fresh dill fronds

Peel the egg and cut it in half lengthwise. Lay the halves in a nest of lettuce. Adorn with olive "eyes," strawberry "beaks," and dill "wings" (as pictured below). If the owls are packed tightly, their features should stay put in transit, but to be safe, you can cover with a folded paper sandwich bag. (We like to tuck a napkin inside the bag in the hope that someone finds it and remembers to use it.)

LOVABLE LEFTOVERS

Sunday nextovers are the unsung heroes of lunchbox prep. Leftovers work best when you use them judiciously, as an intentional main that's nice cold, rather than a last-minute throw-it-in-the-box-and-pray, sorry-it's-weird slapdash save. (Or, worse, last night's rejected dinner rising from the dead to haunt them again.) Start with something they like, which is usually whatever is on heavy rotation for suppers when you have time to cook. For us, that's often pork tenderloin, so this week, leftover slices appear once on their own, more or less like at suppertime, then again tucked into a sandwich. We run that same solo-then-sandwich play for the hard-boiled eggs we usually prep over the weekend.

In the spirit of laudable leftovers, we've filled the rest of the lunchbox compartments with a little bit of a lot of things. We've listed the ingredients in our shopping list, in case you want to replicate these boxes exactly, but our intention is for you to extrapolate these ideas to any bits and bobs kicking around the crisper and deli meat/cheese drawer—the takeaway being that random leftovers can amount to a rad, robust lunch with some five-second food styling. Get into the habit of spotting lunchbox fodder while you're cooking, and cubing/slicing/sequestering them while they're fresh. You'll soon find you're clearing far fewer wilted bell pepper halves, cheese ends, half-full yogurt cups, and past-prime berries from the fridge. This idea goes for the pantry, too, where you'll now see the last five pistachios in the bag and think: lunchbox. The sweet treat this week is inspired by the last gasp of chia seeds in the bottom of a bulk bin bag; they go into a quick (fifteen minutes, start to finish) recipe for healthful Apricot Pistachio Balls. If you make these on Sunday night, they'll last throughout the week. We've tapped them for Monday, Wednesday, and Friday . . . which brings us to our final lesson on leftovers: after a food's third appearance, it's time to move on.

WEEK 2

DAY 1	DAY 2	DAY 3	DAY 4	DAY 5
Minty Mojo	Cubano Club	Olive You, Salami	On a Ham Roll	Fri-yay Face-off

MEAL PREP

SATURDAY
Marinate two **Minty Mojo Pork Tenderloins** (page 104), one for Sunday dinner, one for lunchboxes).

SUNDAY
Roast the **Minty Mojo Pork Tenderloin**.
Make the **Apricot Pistachio Balls** (page 104).
Hard-boil 3 eggs (see page 105).

MONDAY
Make the **Honey Mustard** (page 59), or opt for store-bought and give yourself a night off from lunch prep!

TUESDAY
Prep tomorrow's **Dilly Dip** (page 58).
Practice making tangerine flowers.

WEDNESDAY
Flex your ham and cornichon rolling fingers, then make the roll-ups in the **On a Ham Roll** box (page 112) ahead if you're feeling proactive.

THURSDAY
Prep the filling for tomorrow's **Pickly Egg Salad Sandwich** (page 105) and visualize your sandwich-face-making success.

GROUP PROJECT: All of the recipes this week are well-suited for kid cook collaborators. Mini mathletes who love measuring will enjoy the Minty Mojo Pork Tenderloin, and messy-play pioneers will delight in the Apricot Pistachio Balls, which involve rolling gooey dough into balls and then through shredded coconut. What's not to love, really?

SHOPPING LIST

MEAT + DELI
- [ ] Two 1-pound pork tenderloins (plus more for Sunday supper)
- [ ] ¼ pound deli ham
- [ ] ¼ pound salami

DAIRY CASE
- [ ] 8-ounce block of Swiss cheese
- [ ] 8-ounce block of Cheddar
- [ ] Plain yogurt (you'll need ½ cup)
- [ ] Eggs (you'll need 3)

PRODUCE
- [ ] 3 tangerines
- [ ] 1 orange
- [ ] 1 lemon
- [ ] 1 lime
- [ ] 1 green apple
- [ ] 2 kiwis
- [ ] 1 bunch grapes
- [ ] 1 pint raspberries

- [ ] 1 pint blueberries
- [ ] 1 bag mini sweet peppers
- [ ] ½ pound sugar snap peas
- [ ] 2 carrots
- [ ] 1 bunch radishes
- [ ] 1 head of garlic
- [ ] 1 bunch fresh mint
- [ ] 1 bunch fresh cilantro
- [ ] 1 bunch fresh dill

BREAD + SNACK FOODS
- [ ] 1 bag PopChips
- [ ] 1 box crackers (your choice)
- [ ] 1 loaf sandwich bread

PANTRY + BULK
- [ ] 1 can pitted green olives
- [ ] 1 jar cornichons or pickles
- [ ] ⅓ cup raw almonds
- [ ] ¼ pound roasted unshelled pistachios

- [ ] ¼ pound dried apricots
- [ ] ¼ pound pitted Medjool dates (about 6)
- [ ] ¾ cup unsweetened shredded coconut
- [ ] Fruit snacks and/or roll-ups
- [ ] Mayonnaise
- [ ] Dijon mustard
- [ ] Honey
- [ ] Chia seeds
- [ ] Ground flaxseed
- [ ] Extra-virgin olive oil
- [ ] Ground cumin
- [ ] Kosher salt
- [ ] Black pepper

EXTRA
- [ ] Candy eyeballs (we like Wilton)

CHEAT SHEET: Substitute ¼ pound deli turkey for the pork tenderloin, a jar of (not too spicy) honey mustard for the DIY version, ranch dressing for Dilly Dip, and more dried apricots or fruit bar cookies for the Apricot Pistachio Balls. Make sure you update your shopping list if you choose to swap a store-bought ingredient for a homemade item.

MINTY MOJO PORK TENDERLOIN SERVES 4

⅓ cup packed cilantro sprigs

2 large mint sprigs (about ¼ cup loosely packed)

3 tablespoons fresh orange juice

2 tablespoons fresh lime juice

2 tablespoons extra-virgin olive oil

1 garlic clove

1 teaspoon ground cumin

½ teaspoon kosher salt

¼ teaspoon black pepper

1-pound pork tenderloin

1. Combine the cilantro, mint, orange juice, lime juice, olive oil, garlic, cumin, salt, and pepper in a food processor and process until well blended. Place the tenderloin in a resealable bag, add the marinade, seal shut, and massage until the meat is evenly covered. Let marinate in the refrigerator overnight.

2. Preheat the oven to 350°F.

3. Heat a large cast-iron skillet over medium-high heat, brush with olive oil, and sear the tenderloin until nicely browned, 1 to 2 minutes per side. Cover with foil, transfer to the oven, and roast until an instant-read thermometer registers 145°F, 20 to 25 minutes. Remove from the oven, let sit for 10 minutes, then slice into ½-inch-thick medallions (or bite-size pieces for your youngest lunch buddies). Let cool, then pack in the lunchbox. Store extras in an airtight container in the refrigerator for up to 3 days.

TINY TIP: Zest your orange before juicing it, and use the zest for the Apricot Pistachio Balls (recipe follows).

APRICOT PISTACHIO BALLS MAKES ABOUT 16

⅓ cup shelled roasted pistachios (from about 3 ounces unshelled pistachios)

⅓ cup raw almonds

¼ pound dried apricots (about ½ cup packed)

¼ pound pitted Medjool dates (about 6)

1 tablespoon chia seeds

1 tablespoon ground flaxseed

1 teaspoon grated orange zest

2 teaspoons water

1 cup unsweetened shredded coconut

In a food processor, grind the pistachios and almonds into a coarse meal. Add the apricots, dates, chia seeds, flaxseed, zest, water, and ½ cup of the coconut and process into a sticky paste. Use wet hands to divide the mixture into 16 pieces, then roll each piece into a ball and roll it in the remaining ½ cup coconut. Refrigerate until chilled. Store in an airtight container in the refrigerator for up to 1 week.

THE CRUST CONUNDRUM

If you never cut off the crusts, you will never have to cut off the crusts. If you cut off the crusts once, you will cut them off 100,000 times. However, your crustless sandwiches will look lovely in the lunchbox.

PICKLY EGG SALAD SANDWICH MAKES 1

2 hard-boiled eggs (see below), finely chopped

1 tablespoon finely chopped cornichons or pickles

1 tablespoon mayonnaise

1 teaspoon Dijon mustard

1 teaspoon finely chopped fresh dill

Splash of cornichon or pickle juice

Salt and pepper to taste

2 slices sandwich bread

Various edible facial features (such as sliced green olive eyes, sliced grape nose, radish half-moon smile, sliced mini sweet pepper ears, kiwi triangle eyebrows)

Mix together the chopped eggs, pickles, mayonnaise, mustard, dill, pickle juice, salt, and pepper. Spread the egg salad evenly on a piece of bread, top with the second slice, trim off the crusts if desired, place in the lunchbox, and decorate as shown on page 115, or with your own creative spin.

HOW TO HARD-BOIL AN EGG WITHOUT GETTING BLUE

Using a slotted spoon, gently lower room-temperature eggs into a pot of boiling water. Cook for 13 minutes, adjusting the heat to maintain a gentle boil. Remove the eggs and immediately plunge them into an ice bath for perfectly golden (and gratefully not gray/blue, because there's no way they're eating those) egg yolks.

VARIATION: To make the pretty-in-pink beet-pickled egg shown on page 63, buy a jar of pickled beets, eat the beets, and soak your hard-boiled eggs in the brine overnight. Save this trick for Valentine's Day for maximum shock and awe.

MINTY MOJO

**Sunday supper's leftovers and
Monday's lunchbox were mint to be.**

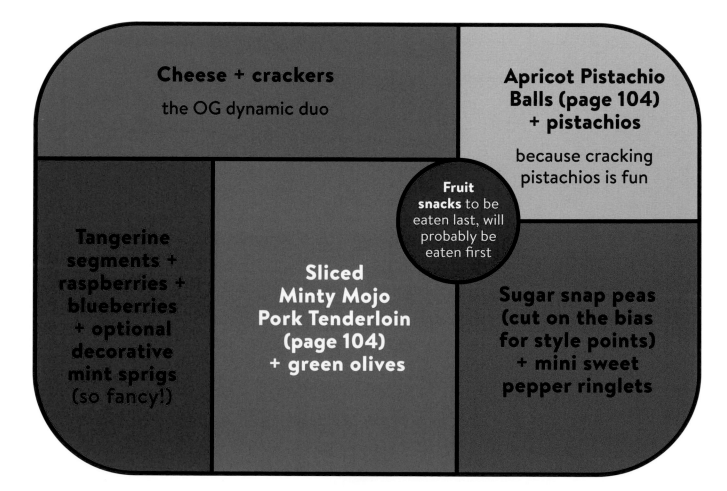

Cheese + crackers

the OG dynamic duo

Apricot Pistachio Balls (page 104) + pistachios

because cracking pistachios is fun

Fruit snacks to be eaten last, will probably be eaten first

Tangerine segments + raspberries + blueberries + optional decorative mint sprigs (so fancy!)

Sliced Minty Mojo Pork Tenderloin (page 104) + green olives

Sugar snap peas (cut on the bias for style points) + mini sweet pepper ringlets

CUBANO CLUB

**Take an ordinary ham sam to new heights
(but not so high it won't fit in a small mouth).**

Cubano club sandwich

= honey mustard
(store-bought or homemade,
page 59) + chopped
or sliced cornichons +
sliced pork tenderloin +
sliced ham + sliced
Swiss cheese

Optional cornichon on top,
because the only thing better
than a pickle is a tiny pickle

Strategic PopChip placement
prevents sandwich shiftage and
crunch shortage

**Kiwi half-moons +
halved grapes**

Fruit
Roll-up
in the
middle

**Sugar snap peas,
cut on the bias +
carrot curls cut with
a vegetable peeler**

(because you could have
carrot coins OR you could
have carrot *curls*)

OLIVE YOU, SALAMI

**Add a little pizzazz to this classic combo
and practice your AB patterns.**

Mini sweet pepper ringlets + carrot coins + radishes cut in half

Apricot Pistachio Balls (page 104)

in a shredded coconut nest

Tangerine *Flowers* with a grape center + mint leaves (obviously overkill, but awfully cute)

Salami and green olive mini skewers + Swiss cheese cubes

Hard-boiled egg **(see page 105)** with eyeballs (because absolutely everything is better with candy eyeballs) + **store-bought ranch dressing or homemade Dilly Dip (page 58)**

MEET YOUR MEAT

The loose-tooth set often prefers lunch meat *sans* the sandwich. That's where you come in.

CUBE IT: Order a 1½-inch-thick slab of turkey or ham at the deli counter and slice into cubes.

FOLD IT: Fold a salami slice into quarters and skewer with olives, cheese, or cherry tomatoes.

SPIRAL IT: Spread a slice of any deli meat with a soft cheese (such as cream cheese), roll it up, and slice it into bites.

RIBBON IT: Cut a slice of deli meat lengthwise into 1½-inch strips. Gently fold each ribbon accordion-style into an S-shape, then skewer it.

BUNCH IT: Tear thinly sliced prosciutto into smaller pieces and bunch together in little bites, **EAT IT.**

ON A HAM ROLL

Because tiny pickles are fun, and so is having at least twelve different things in one lunchbox.

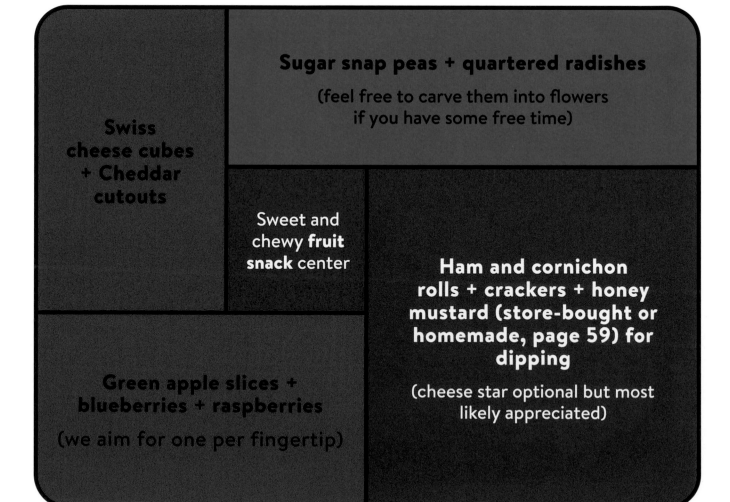

Swiss cheese cubes + Cheddar cutouts

Sugar snap peas + quartered radishes

(feel free to carve them into flowers if you have some free time)

Sweet and chewy **fruit snack** center

Ham and cornichon rolls + crackers + honey mustard (store-bought or homemade, page 59) for dipping

(cheese star optional but most likely appreciated)

Green apple slices + blueberries + raspberries

(we aim for one per fingertip)

FRI-YAY FACE-OFF

Give the classic egg salad sandwich a fresh-dill-and-pickle punch-up plus a little personality.

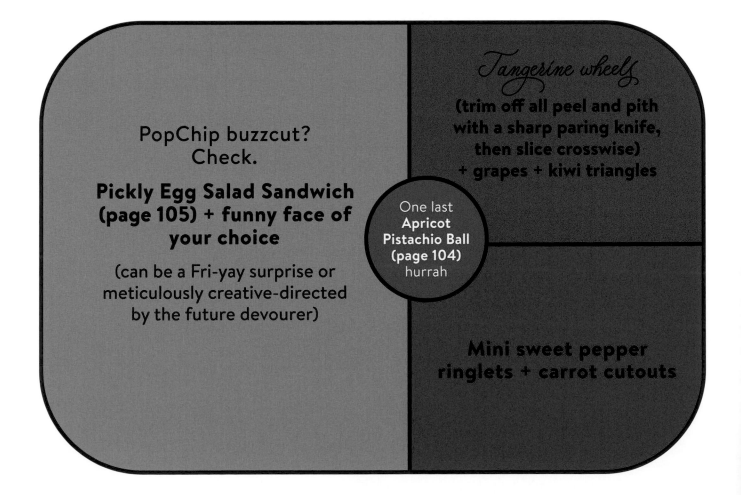

PopChip buzzcut? Check.

Pickly Egg Salad Sandwich (page 105) + funny face of your choice

(can be a Fri-yay surprise or meticulously creative-directed by the future devourer)

Tangerine wheels

(trim off all peel and pith with a sharp paring knife, then slice crosswise) + grapes + kiwi triangles

One last **Apricot Pistachio Ball (page 104)** hurrah

Mini sweet pepper ringlets + carrot cutouts

DUMPLING YOU SHOULD KNOW

This week we're taking our cue from a four-year-old with a penchant for potstickers, who never met a dumpling he didn't like, and whose only question upon seeing four gyoza in his lunchbox was why aren't there ten, and also where's the bao? (It's on page 69, little friend.)

You can pick up a bag of gyoza in the freezer section or take on the DIY version for quality family kitchen time. When you have many little fingers ready to pleat, pleat, pleat before they eat, eat, eat, it's a party (also, a nice no-eye-contact opening to chat about whatever is on their mind). If there's only enough time for eating, not pleating, buy them frozen and give them a quick steam before building the lunchbox. And, yes, you can plunk them directly in the box, rather than showing up in the cafetorium with your steaming basket and piping-hot gyoza. Of the many peculiarities of children, one that lunchbox packers can benefit from is their total indifference to room-temperature food. If you happen to have a middle schooler who likes it hot, pack the dumplings in a thermos container or a hybrid lunchbox-thermos container (it's amazing; see page 77).

We round out our bundles of joy with more fun Asian-inspired flavors and tantalizing textures, starting with an easy-to-toss-together peanut noodle salad. Be sure to pack training chopsticks or a fork to accompany this dish, and further help the littlest lunchers by cutting up the noodles with scissors. And while we're on the subject of neater eaters, when tofu-and-edamame day (a.k.a. Day 3: Soy into You) rolls around, we recommend packing a bento fork for keeping all soy sauce dunking splash-free. For extra assurance against spillage, schlep said soy sauce in a tiny squeeze container—lest it infiltrate the Matcha Milk Pudding, which would be very sad, and we'd far prefer to end the week on a Summer Roll high.

WEEK 3

DAY 1	DAY 2	DAY 3	DAY 4	DAY 5
Peas Pass the Noodles	Filling Good	Soy into You	Here We Gyoza Again	Summer Roll Model

MEAL PREP

SUNDAY

Make **Peanut Noodles** (page 120), reserving 2 tablespoons of the peanut sauce for Friday's dip. Make **Cucumber Sesame Salad** (page 121). Throw a **Ginger Pork Gyoza** gathering (page 120) . . . or buy a bag of gyoza. Plunk frozen edamame in the lunchbox; they'll thaw by lunch.

MONDAY

Bake **Lemon Poppyseed Mini Muffins** (page 121) after school. Make **Matcha Milk Pudding** (page 122) and pour into two separate lunchboxes to set.

Make **Dumpling Dipping Sauce** (page 123) and store it in two small containers. Steam **Ginger Pork Gyoza**; if panfrying, wait until the morning to prepare.

TUESDAY

Prep the **Surprise Party Popcorn** (page 122).

WEDNESDAY

Steam dumplings or, if panfrying, wait until the morning to prepare.

THURSDAY

Make **Tofu Summer Rolls** (page 123) and pack with a damp paper towel on top.

GROUP PROJECT: If we've said it once, we've said it thrice: a dumpling night is a superb way to spend family time. If you haven't the time or the inclination, Lemon Poppyseed Mini Muffins are a good go-to. If your sous chef is impatient and perhaps could use a snack, then it's Surprise Party Popcorn for you—the recipe makes more than you'll need for the lunchbox.

MEAT + DELI

- [ ] ½ pound ground pork

DAIRY CASE

- [ ] 1 block firm tofu
- [ ] Half-and-half or whole milk (you'll need 1 cup)
- [ ] Plain yogurt (you'll need ⅓ cup)
- [ ] Eggs (you'll need 1)

PRODUCE

- [ ] 3 carrots
- [ ] 1 pound Persian cucumbers, plus 1 cuke for the Summer Roll
- [ ] 1 bunch scallions
- [ ] 1 head of garlic
- [ ] 1 piece fresh ginger
- [ ] 2 tangerines
- [ ] 1 lemon
- [ ] 1 lime
- [ ] 1 pint raspberries
- [ ] 1 small head green cabbage
- [ ] Handful of fresh spinach
- [ ] 1 bunch fresh mint
- [ ] 1 bunch fresh cilantro

BREAD + SNACK FOODS

- [ ] 1 bag (less spicy) rice cracker mix
- [ ] 1 bag dried apple chips

PANTRY + BULK

- [ ] 1 cup brown rice flour
- [ ] ⅓ cup popcorn kernels
- [ ] 1 tablespoon peanuts
- [ ] Rice paper wrappers (about 8½ inches in diameter)
- [ ] Matcha green tea powder
- [ ] Xanthan gum
- [ ] Yellow gel food coloring (optional)
- [ ] Kosher salt

- [ ] Baking powder
- [ ] Baking soda
- [ ] Granulated sugar
- [ ] Light soy sauce
- [ ] ½ cup creamy peanut butter
- [ ] Honey
- [ ] Rice vinegar
- [ ] Toasted sesame oil
- [ ] White sesame seeds
- [ ] Poppy seeds
- [ ] Coconut oil
- [ ] Coconut milk (you'll need 2 tablespoons)
- [ ] Safflower or other neutral oil
- [ ] 1 package udon-style noodles
- [ ] 1 packet unflavored gelatin

FREEZER

- [ ] 1 bag unshelled edamame
- [ ] Gyoza wrappers

EXTRA

- [ ] 1 box chocolate button candies, such as M&M's
- [ ] 1 box Pocky

CHEAT SHEET: Substitute premade pudding, a jar of peanut sauce, sesame noodles from the deli case, frozen gyoza, a bag of popcorn, store-bought mini muffins, a summer roll from your favorite Southeast Asian restaurant (and, yes, you should pick up take-out for dinner) for the recipes that follow. Make sure you update your shopping list if you choose to swap a store-bought ingredient for a homemade item.

PEANUT NOODLES   MAKES 3 SERVINGS

6 ounces udon-style noodles

3 tablespoons Peanut Sauce (page 59, or store-bought)

¼ cup shredded carrots

½ scallion, thinly sliced on the bias

1 tablespoon crushed peanuts

1. Prepare the noodles according to the package instructions.
2. Gently toss the cooked noodles with the peanut sauce, carrots, and scallion until combined. Transfer to the lunchbox and garnish with crushed peanuts.

VARIATION: *If your school is nut-free, toss noodles in a splash of soy sauce and toasted sesame oil instead.*

GINGER PORK GYOZA   MAKE5 ABOUT 25

2 cups finely chopped or grated green cabbage

2 teaspoons kosher salt

½ pound ground pork

¼ cup thinly sliced scallions

1 tablespoon grated peeled fresh ginger

1 teaspoon grated garlic

1 teaspoon lightsoy sauce

½ teaspoon toasted sesame oil

25 gyoza wrappers

Vegetable or avocado oil (optional)

1. Toss the cabbage with the salt in a large bowl, let sit for 15 minutes, then gently squeeze dry with a clean kitchen towel. Add the pork, scallions, ginger, garlic, soy sauce, and sesame oil and mix together.
2. Spoon a scant tablespoon of the filling into the center of each dumpling wrapper, then dip a finger in water and run it around the edge of the wrapper to moisten it. Fold the wrapper in half (like a taco), and use your thumb and forefinger to pleat and press the dumpling shut.
3. To fry the dumplings: Heat 1 to 2 tablespoons of vegetable oil in a large lidded nonstick skillet over medium-high heat, until hot but not smoking. Add half the dumplings and fry until the bottoms are golden brown, 2 to 3 minutes. Add ½ cup water, cover the skillet, and cook until the water has evaporated and the dumplings are cooked through, about 5 minutes. (Cut one open to make sure it's done.) Take off the lid, shake the skillet to loosen up the dumplings, and let the bottoms re-crisp, 1 to 2 minutes. Repeat with the remaining dumplings.

4. To steam the dumplings: Steam them in a bamboo or stainless-steel steamer lined with parchment paper until cooked through, about 10 minutes.
5. Tuck the cooked gyoza into a thermos container, or cool and pack in the lunchbox.
6. Extra dumplings can be placed on a parchment-lined sheet pan (don't let them touch), frozen until firm, then transferred to a resealable container and frozen for up to 1 month.

LEMON POPPYSEED MINI MUFFINS MAKES 24

¾ cup plus 2 tablespoons brown rice flour
⅔ cup sugar
¾ teaspoon xanthan gum
½ teaspoon baking powder
½ teaspoon kosher salt
¼ teaspoon baking soda
½ cup neutral oil (such as safflower or vegetable oil)
⅓ cup plain yogurt
1 large egg
1 tablespoon poppy seeds
2 teaspoons grated lemon zest
2 tablespoons fresh lemon juice
⅛ teaspoon yellow gel food coloring (optional)

1. Preheat the oven to 350°F and position an oven rack in the center. Spray a 24-cup mini-muffin pan with baking spray or line the cups with mini-muffin papers.
2. Combine the flour, sugar, xanthan gum, baking powder, salt, and baking soda in a large bowl and stir to combine. Make a well in the center and add the oil, yogurt, egg, poppy seeds, lemon zest, lemon juice, and food coloring (if using). Stir until fully incorporated. Set aside to rest for 30 minutes.
3. Use a 1½-inch scoop or spoon to distribute the batter evenly among the muffin cups. Bake for 12 to 15 minutes, until the edges turn golden and a tester comes out clean. Let cool and pack in the lunchbox.

CUCUMBER SESAME SALAD MAKES 4 SERVINGS

1 pound Persian cucumbers, split vertically and sliced into 1-inch segments
Kosher salt
3 tablespoons rice vinegar
2 tablespoons neutral oil (such as safflower or vegetable)
1 tablespoon light soy sauce
2 teaspoons toasted sesame oil
½ teaspoon sugar
1 tablespoon white sesame seeds

1. Combine the cucumbers with a large pinch of salt and set in a colander to drain for 15 minutes. Pat dry with a paper towel. In a large (5-cup or more) airtight container, add the rice vinegar, neutral oil, soy sauce, sesame oil, and sugar. Cover and shake to combine. Add the cucumbers to the container, and shake again. Sprinkle with the sesame seeds.
2. The salad will keep in the refrigerator for 3 days.

SURPRISE PARTY POPCORN SERVES 4

2 tablespoons coconut oil or neutral oil (such as safflower or vegetable oil)

⅓ cup popcorn kernels

Kosher salt

Chocolate button candies, such as Smarties or M&M's

Melt the oil in a large pot with a tight-fitting lid over high heat. Add the popcorn kernels and cover the pot. When the first kernel pops, pull the pot from the heat, give it a good swirl, and return it to the burner. Repeat every 10 seconds or so, until the popping slows to a pop every few seconds, then remove the pot from heat. Sprinkle with salt, toss, and sprinkle with more salt. Cool the popcorn, then scoop it into the lunchbox along with a handful of chocolate Smarties or M&M's.

VARIATION: *To make the Sprinkle Popcorn seen on the cover, place 3 cups of popcorn in a large bowl and drizzle with 1 ounce melted white chocolate. Stir with a nonstick spatula to coat. Spread the popcorn on a sheet pan in a single layer and sprinkle generously with sprinkles. Let cool completely before scooping into a lunchbox. Best eaten within 1 day.*

MATCHA MILK PUDDING SERVES 2

1 cup half-and-half or whole milk

3 tablespoons sugar

1 teaspoon matcha green tea powder

1 teaspoon unflavored gelatin, such as Knox

Raspberries, decorating sugar, or sprinkles (optional)

1. Combine the half-and-half, sugar, and matcha in a small pot over medium heat and sprinkle the gelatin on top. Cook for about 3 minutes, stirring often, just until bubbles begin to form around the edge of the pot and the sugar dissolves. Remove from heat.

2. Set a fine-mesh strainer over a spouted measuring cup and strain the pudding. Pour into two ½-cup lidded metal ramekins or the ½-cup compartments of two leakproof lunchboxes. (If using a plastic lunchbox, cool the pudding on the counter for 10 minutes, skim the top if necessary, then pour into the ½-cup compartment.) Refrigerate overnight to set.

3. Before sending to school, garnish with raspberries, decorating sugar, or sprinkles, if you like.

TOFU SUMMER ROLL MAKES 1 ROLL

1 small thick carrot, peeled
½ small Persian cucumber
1 rice paper wrapper
4 large mint leaves
Handful of fresh spinach
    (or greens of choice)

2 cilantro sprigs
Firm tofu, cut into
    a ½-inch-thick
    5-inch-long stick

1. Cut four ⅛-inch-thick slices from the thickest part of the carrot and use a 1-inch food cutter to stamp out stars, flowers, bears, or whatever shape will be a surefire hit. Cut the rest of the carrot and the cucumber into matchsticks (or use a julienne peeler). Soak the rice paper wrapper in a pie dish filled with warm water until pliable, about 5 seconds. Transfer to a sheet of parchment paper.

2. Place the four cutouts in a row, spaced out a bit, on the bottom half of the wrapper, leaving room on both sides. Lay the mint leaves diagonally over the top to cover (this is strictly for aesthetic purposes; it'll also be fine if you forgo the cutout art project and just pile everything in there). Pile the spinach, cilantro, carrot and cucumber matchsticks, and tofu in a row on top (don't overstuff, or the roll will make like your pants after Thanksgiving dinner and split).

3. Roll one full turn, carefully tucking in the ingredients. Fold in both sides of the wrapper. Continue rolling, burrito/wrap/strudel-style, keeping everything tucked in snugly. Cut in half, on an angle, place in the lunchbox, and cover with a damp paper towel. If not serving immediately, wrap the roll securely in plastic wrap and store in the refrigerator for up to 1 day.

DUMPLING DIPPING SAUCE

Mix one part soy sauce to one part rice vinegar (to prevent spillage, sequester the dipping sauce in a small airtight container or bottle; easily found online).

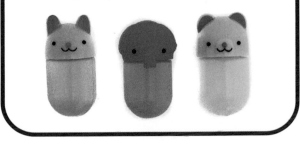

PEAS PASS THE NOODLES

Saucy Peanut Noodles, crunchy rice cracker mix, three fun fruits, and a built-in activity: pinching open those glorious green edamame pods.

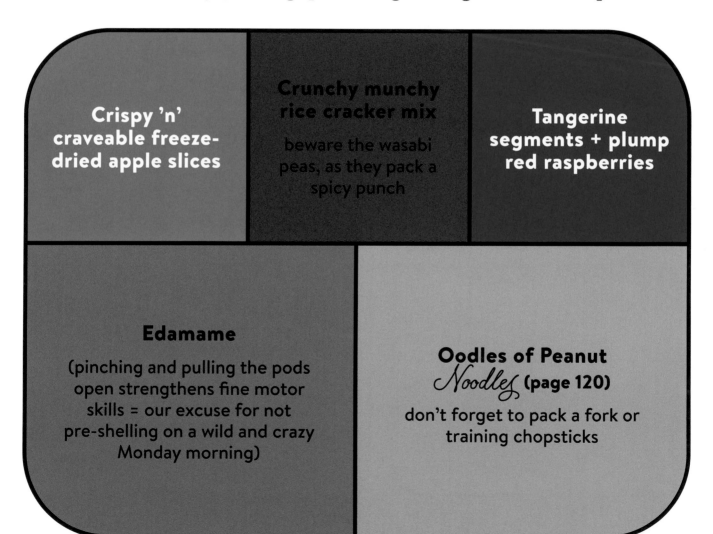

Crispy 'n' craveable freeze-dried apple slices

Crunchy munchy rice cracker mix

beware the wasabi peas, as they pack a spicy punch

Tangerine segments + plump red raspberries

Edamame

(pinching and pulling the pods open strengthens fine motor skills = our excuse for not pre-shelling on a wild and crazy Monday morning)

Oodles of Peanut *Noodles* **(page 120)**

don't forget to pack a fork or training chopsticks

CAFETERIA DUTY DOS AND DON'TS

Look at you, doing your part to keep the cafeteria calm! According to PTA presidents we know and love, please don't forget the following.

1. Arrive early. School parking is unpredictable.
2. Wear gloves (they're often available in the cafeteria).
3. Brush up on your string-cheese-opening skills.
4. Mingle and make conversation; kids are more likely to ask for help if you're already chatting.
5. When you can't get a word out of anyone, ask what they like to do at recess.
6. Kids misbehave when they're bored. Start a game of "I Spy" or a joke contest if you see signs of mischief-making. (Have a couple of kid-friendly jokes in your back pocket.)
7. Be efficient! The time goes by quickly.

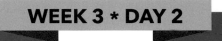
FILLING GOOD

Pleat, eat, what a treat (especially when partnered with a quick and creamy Matcha Milk Pudding for dessert).

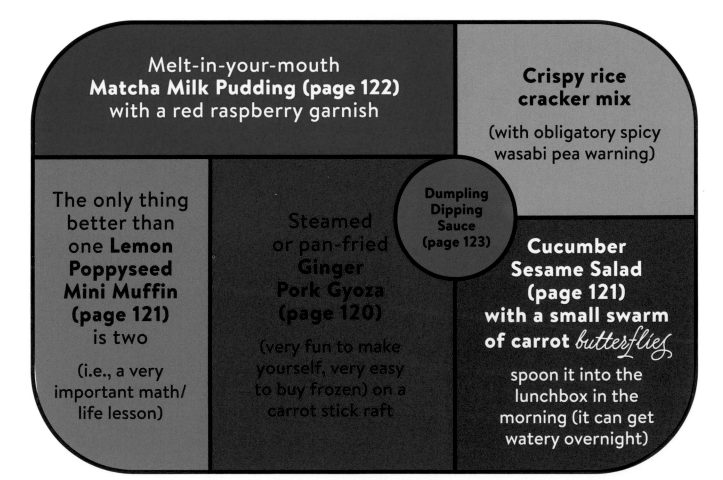

Melt-in-your-mouth **Matcha Milk Pudding (page 122)** with a red raspberry garnish

Crispy rice cracker mix

(with obligatory spicy wasabi pea warning)

The only thing better than one **Lemon Poppyseed Mini Muffin (page 121)** is two

(i.e., a very important math/ life lesson)

Steamed or pan-fried **Ginger Pork Gyoza (page 120)**

(very fun to make yourself, very easy to buy frozen) on a carrot stick raft

Dumpling Dipping Sauce (page 123)

Cucumber Sesame Salad (page 121) with a small swarm of carrot *butterflies*

spoon it into the lunchbox in the morning (it can get watery overnight)

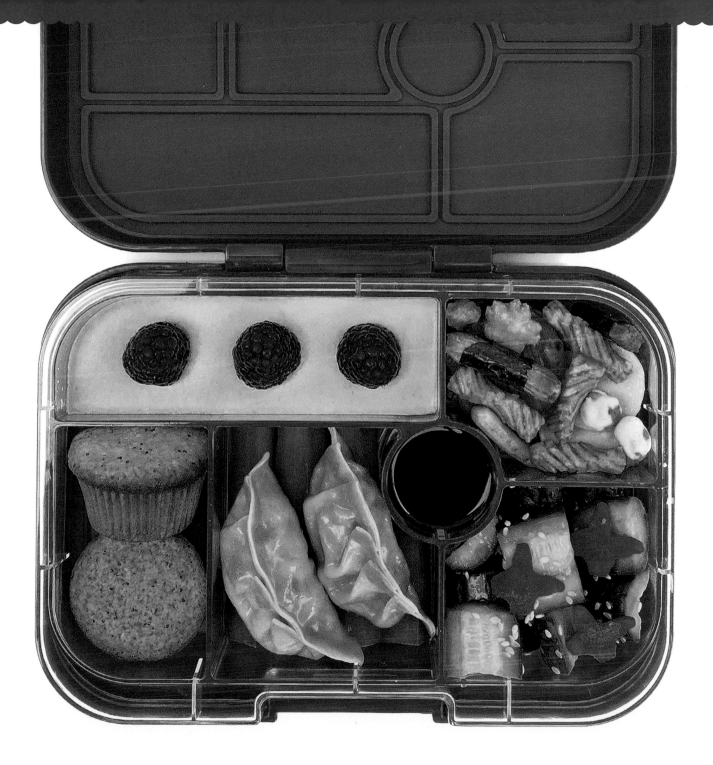

SOY INTO YOU

Creamy tofu cubes are the star of this lunchtime revue, but the chocolate button candies hidden in the popcorn will probably steal the show.

Surprise Party Popcorn (page 122) with a chocolate button candy color pop

(can double as a family movie night snack)

Matcha Milk Pudding (page 122) with sprinkles on top

(because we love any excuse for sprinkles on top)

Cucumber Sesame Salad (page 121)

scooped into the lunchbox with a slotted spoon

Cubes of firm tofu + shelled edamame

(we exercised great restraint using only one bento pick; feel free to poke one into every cube—it's a great stress reliever)

Dumpling Dipping Sauce (page 123)

The prettiest tangerine on the tree

(or in the box)

HERE WE GYOZA AGAIN

These dumplings are so nice, we're eating them twice (this time
with a Pocky stick dessert/appetizer; could go either way).

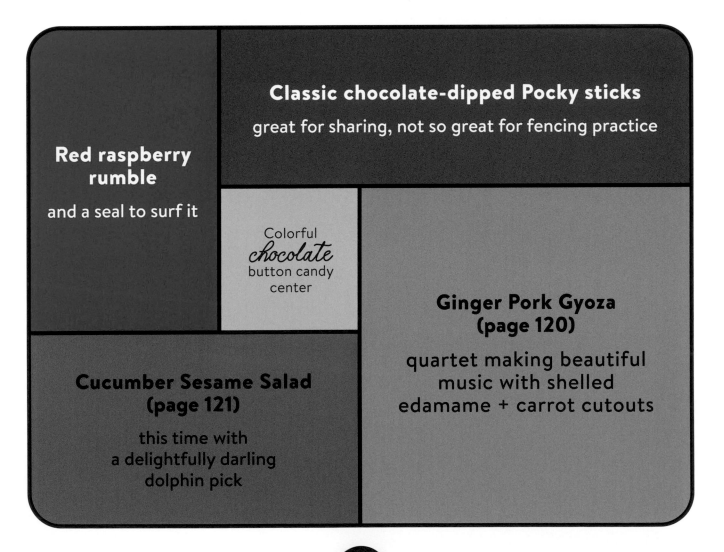

Classic chocolate-dipped Pocky sticks

great for sharing, not so great for fencing practice

Red raspberry rumble

and a seal to surf it

Colorful *chocolate* button candy center

Ginger Pork Gyoza (page 120)

quartet making beautiful music with shelled edamame + carrot cutouts

Cucumber Sesame Salad (page 121)

this time with a delightfully darling dolphin pick

SUMMER ROLL MODEL

Bright, beautiful tofu-and-vegetable summer rolls are an edible garden party in a box. Tuck them in for the night (or morning) with a damp paper towel on top to keep the rolls fresh until lunchtime.

Tofu Summer Rolls (page 123)

one whole, with strategically placed carrot cutouts for maximum wow factor; one cut into quarters and positioned upright for a sneak preview of what's inside

And for extra credit, an unnecessary but very fetching fresh mint and cilantro garnish

Peanut Sauce (page 59, or store-bought)

Lemon Poppyseed Mini Muffin (page 121)

twinsies for dessert

Rice cracker snack mix

if we've said it once, we've said it three times (well, in this chapter, anyway): those wasabi peas can pack a spicy wallop, so pluck them out if need be

132

LET'S NOODLE ON IT

Hey, Mom-bo (and Dad-bo), we're going Italian-o this week, with easy peas-y Presto Pesto pasta salad, ham-wrapped grissini breadsticks, and a salami rose worthy of the Uffizi. This whirlwind tour begins on Sunday, when you'll start forming the life-changing habit of clearing up one meal (dinner) while packing another (lunch). Stir what's left of dinner's veggies into a fresh batch of Lemony Pearl Couscous (a.k.a. "tiny pasta balls"), tuck a reserved piece of protein into the main lunchbox compartment, and add a fruit skewer and some crunchy crackers.

Tuesday's lunchbox smuggles veggies by way of spinach-stuffed tortellini and chicken-zucchini meatballs, two foods we always keep in the freezer because they're easy to make in individual portions. Then, Wednesday's box brings the fun. Warm up by making a pattern with melon bites using a circle-shaped food cutter (active time: 30 seconds), then take it up a notch by chiseling wax-covered Babybel cheeses into works of carved perfection

(active time: varies by talent/perfectionism; it took Michelangelo two years to complete *David* . . . just saying), or use your 1-inch food cutters to simply punch a shape out of the wax (see page 33 for examples).

Thursday's lunchbox dishes up many kids' forever-favorite dish: noodles. Barilla's "mini" series is just the right size for the little guys. If you substitute Banza's chickpea wheels to pack in a little more protein, rinse them well after cooking for a less-likely-to-be-rejected texture. In the spirit of surefire hits, we also snuck a pocket-size toy into lunch this week. While this isn't sanctioned, strictly speaking, we've never been busted for it. And while we're on the subject of breaking the rules, who says charcuterie boards are just for grown-ups? Whenever you're planning to make party snacks over the weekend, save yourself some extra meal-planning and snag some of your supplies for Friday's lunchbox. Buon appetito, bambini!

WEEK 4

DAY 1 Salmon Supper, Take Two	**DAY 2** It's Pasta Your Lunchtime	**DAY 3** Having a Ball	**DAY 4** Wheel Good Food	**DAY 5** Roman Friday

MEAL PREP

SUNDAY

Snag a piece of grilled salmon (or whatever you're eating for dinner) for Monday's lunchbox.
Make **Lemony Pearl Couscous** (page 139). Make **Chicken and Zucchini Mini Meatballs** (page 139). Make **Presto Pesto** (page 52) or buy a jar; pack some into a small lidded container for Tuesday's lunchbox, and save some to mix into the pasta wheels Wednesday night.

MONDAY

Skewer the tortellini and caprese salad, using the picture on page 143 as a guide. Snip off the skewers' pointy ends with garden shears if your kids are little.

TUESDAY

Skewer the **Chicken and Zucchini Mini Meatballs** and cherry tomatoes (see page 145). Punch out melon circles using a 1-inch food cutter. Make four cheesy-on-the-eyes Babybels (see page 33) and store them in an airtight container in the refrigerator.

WEDNESDAY

Bake the **Three-Bite Brownies** (page 138). Stir your pesto into pasta.

THURSDAY

Punch out melon butterflies using a 1-inch food cutter. Make a **salami rose** (page 149) and build tomorrow's charcuterie box.

GROUP PROJECT: Bake the Three-Bite Brownies with your resident dessert nibbler. It's all too easy to polish off the batch, so be sure to set aside three for the lunchbox as soon as they're cool (not that we're speaking from experience or anything).

SHOPPING LIST

MEAT + DELI

- [ ] ½ pound ground chicken
- [ ] ¼ pound thinly sliced salami
- [ ] ¼ pound thinly sliced ham

DAIRY CASE

- [ ] 1 stick unsalted butter
- [ ] Eggs (you'll need 4)
- [ ] 1 bag Mini Babybel cheeses
- [ ] 1 (8-ounce) tub mini mozzarella balls (ciliegine)
- [ ] 4 ounces Parmigiano-Reggiano
- [ ] 1 package tortellini

PRODUCE

- [ ] 1 bunch grapes
- [ ] 1 small cantaloupe
- [ ] 1 small watermelon
- [ ] 1 head of garlic
- [ ] 4 lemons
- [ ] 2 zucchini, grated (2 cups)

- [ ] 1 bunch asparagus
- [ ] 1 pint cherry tomatoes
- [ ] 1 shallot
- [ ] 1 bunch fresh basil
- [ ] 1 bunch fresh mint
- [ ] 1 bunch fresh parsley

BREAD + SNACK FOODS

- [ ] 1 box club crackers
- [ ] 1 box mini fruit-and-nut crisps
- [ ] 1 box grissini breadsticks

PANTRY + BULK

- [ ] ¼ cup Guara or Marcona almonds
- [ ] 1 can pitted green olives (or 5 olives from olive bar)
- [ ] 1½ cups or 1 (8-ounce) bag Israeli couscous
- [ ] 1 box wagon wheel (mini rotelle) pasta
- [ ] ½ cup bittersweet chocolate chips

- [ ] 1 bag freeze-dried strawberries
- [ ] Extra-virgin olive oil
- [ ] Sugar
- [ ] All-purpose flour
- [ ] Unsweetened cocoa powder
- [ ] Pure vanilla extract
- [ ] Kosher salt and black pepper
- [ ] Chicken broth
- [ ] Breadcrumbs
- [ ] Garlic powder
- [ ] Onion powder

FREEZER

- [ ] 1 bag frozen peas

EXTRA

- [ ] Leftover protein portion from supper
- [ ] Candy eyeballs
- [ ] Gummy bears
- [ ] Quadratini wafer cookies

CHEAT SHEET:
To buy instead of DIY, purchase premade mini brownies, a container of store-bought pesto, a pint of grain salad (to substitute for couscous, or make more tortellini), and a bag of mini meatballs from the freezer section. Make sure you update your shopping list if you choose to swap a store-bought ingredient for a homemade item.

THREE-BITE BROWNIES MAKES 24

4 tablespoons (½ stick) unsalted
   butter, plus more for greasing

¼ cup extra-virgin olive oil

1 cup sugar

2 large eggs

2 teaspoons pure vanilla extract

½ teaspoon kosher salt

⅔ cup unsweetened cocoa powder,
   sifted

½ cup all-purpose flour

½ cup bittersweet chocolate chips

1. Preheat the oven to 350°F. Generously grease a 24-cup mini muffin pan with butter (or line with mini muffin wrappers).
2. Melt together the butter and olive oil in a small saucepan until very hot. In a medium bowl, whisk together the sugar, eggs, vanilla, and salt until smooth and pale yellow, about 2 minutes. Whisking continuously, slowly stream the hot butter-oil mixture into the egg mixture. Mix in the cocoa powder and flour until just combined, then stir in the chocolate chips.
3. Use a small cookie scoop to fill each muffin cup with batter. Bake the brownies until the tops look dry and crackly and the center is firm but still moist, 10 to 12 minutes. Let the brownies cool for 5 minutes in the pan, then transfer them to a wire rack to cool completely before packing in the lunchbox. Store in an airtight container at room temperature for up to 3 days or in the freezer for up to 1 month; remove in the morning and let thaw in the lunchbox.

LEMONY PEARL COUSCOUS SERVES 6

⅓ cup extra-virgin olive oil

1 teaspoon grated lemon zest

⅓ cup fresh lemon juice

2 tablespoons unsalted butter

1 large shallot, finely chopped

1½ cups pearl (Israeli) couscous

½ teaspoon kosher salt

1¾ cups low-sodium chicken or
  vegetable broth

½ bunch asparagus, stems split
  vertically and cut into 2-inch segments
  (optional)

½ cup frozen peas, thawed (optional)

¼ cup finely chopped fresh mint

1. Whisk together the olive oil, lemon zest, and lemon juice in a small bowl. Set aside.
2. Melt the butter in a large saucepan over medium-low heat and cook the shallot, stirring often, until soft but not brown, about 3 minutes. Add the couscous and salt and cook until the couscous turns golden, about 5 minutes. Add the broth and bring to a boil. Reduce heat to low, cover, and simmer until the broth has been absorbed and the couscous is tender, about 10 minutes. In the last 2 minutes, add the asparagus and peas to the pot, if using. (Or omit asparagus and peas and use 2 cups of any leftover bite-size steamed vegetables you have on hand.)
3. Transfer to a large bowl and toss with the reserved dressing and the mint. Cool and spoon into the lunchbox. Store leftovers in the refrigerator for up to 5 days.

CHICKEN AND ZUCCHINI MINI MEATBALLS MAKES 40 (YES, 40; THEY'RE TEENY)

1 zucchini, grated (about 1 cup)

½ pound ground chicken or turkey

1 large egg, lightly beaten

½ cup breadcrumbs

¼ cup grated Parmigiano-Reggiano

¾ teaspoon kosher salt

½ teaspoon garlic powder

½ teaspoon onion powder

2 tablespoons finely chopped fresh
  parsley

Extra-virgin olive oil

1. Preheat the oven to 425°F. Line a sheet pan with parchment paper.
2. Wrap the grated zucchini in a clean kitchen towel and gently squeeze to remove excess moisture, then place in a large bowl. Add the chicken, egg, breadcrumbs, cheese, salt, garlic powder, onion powder, and parsley and mix together with clean hands. Chill in the refrigerator for 15 minutes.
3. Use a melon baller or a rounded teaspoon to scoop the meatball mixture into clean, wet hands. Form into meatballs and place 1 inch apart on the prepared pan. Brush tops with olive oil. Bake for 10 to 12 minutes, until cooked through and beginning to brown. Let cool, then transfer the meatballs to the lunchbox or an airtight container. Store in the refrigerator for up to 3 days or the freezer for up to a month.

SALMON SUPPER, TAKE TWO

Since last night's fintastic Sunday Salmon Supper went so
swimmingly, you scale up and serve it for lunch, too.
(Sorry, but who can resist a fish pun? Not us.)

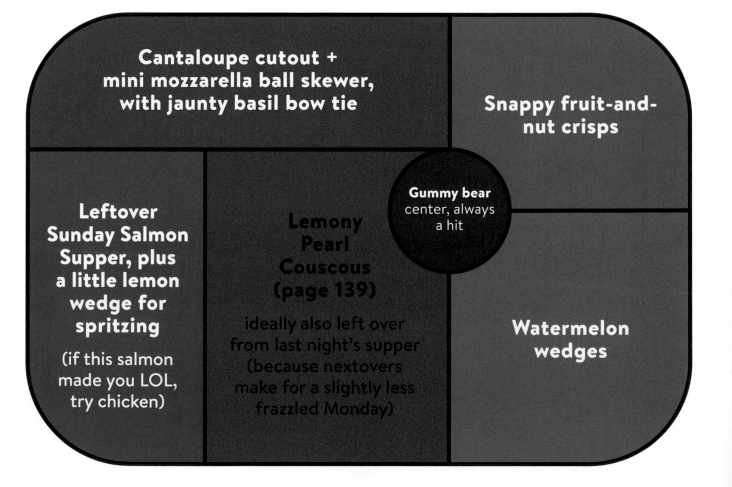

Cantaloupe cutout +
mini mozzarella ball skewer,
with jaunty basil bow tie

Snappy fruit-and-
nut crisps

Leftover
Sunday Salmon
Supper, plus
a little lemon
wedge for
spritzing

(if this salmon
made you LOL,
try chicken)

Lemony
Pearl
Couscous
(page 139)

ideally also left over
from last night's supper
(because nextovers
make for a slightly less
frazzled Monday)

Gummy bear
center, always
a hit

Watermelon
wedges

IT'S PASTA YOUR LUNCHTIME

Teeny tortellini and caprese with a chance of meatballs.

TEENY
Tortellini
skewers + a cherry tomato, basil, and mini mozzarella ball skewer

A cup of Presto Pesto (page 52, or store-bought) for dipping, with a side of crunchy Guara or Marcona almonds

Bite-size **chocolate wafer cookies,** such as Quadratini

Peep this heap of **Chicken and Zucchini Mini Meatballs (page 139)**

HAVING A BALL

Yesterday's couscous salad meets today's chicken-zucchini meatball skewer, with a surprise appearance by a mystery guest living everyone's worst school nightmare—forgetting to wear pants.

Watermelon and cantaloupe rounds

= good patterns practice (use a round 1-inch food cutter for this 30-second upgrade)

Chicken and Zucchini Mini Meatballs (page 139) + cherry tomato skewer

What lunch *can't* be improved by **a mini cheese wheel wearing underpants?** (see page 33 for a lesson)

Two Three-Bite Brownies (page 138)

One last hurrah for the **Lemony Pearl Couscous** (page 139) made with peas and asparagus

WHEEL GOOD FOOD

Toss pesto with pasta and peas, craft some quick melon and ham curls, brew a shot of espresso, and flex your cheese-wax-carving fingers.

Cantaloupe and ham curls? What is this, the St. Regis Rome?!

To make, use a Y-peeler to cut ribbons of cantaloupe and roll into a rosette; all the ham slices need is a quick crumple.

Light and crispy freeze-dried strawberries + a chewy chocolate-chip-studded Three-Bite Brownie (page 138) = dessert heaven

A surprise o'saurus

A pair of very fierce miniature cheese wheels

(thank you, trusty X-Acto knife and our dear friend Candy Eyeballs; see page 22)

Wagon wheel pasta and frozen peas tossed with pesto (homemade, page 52, or store-bought) and garnished with fresh basil

TINY TIP:
To make luscious cantaloupe curls, seed and quarter a melon, trim off the rind, and shave the side of the melon wedge with a sharp vegetable peeler, like you're peeling a carrot. Roll the thin strips of melon into curls, and you're done. As for the ham, take each piece and scrunch it 'til it looks fancy. That's it!

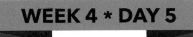

ROMAN FRIDAY

Because opening your lunchbox to see a scrumptious salami rose is nearly as exciting as a scooter ride around Rome.

Very cute Vespa napkin which prompts a game of "What's wrong with this picture?" (Hint: We fell behind on Duolingo.)

Babybel, turned into nature's luckiest lady (see page 33) with the help of a black olive and candy eyeballs; on a club cracker stacker

A bitty bunch of sweet, *juicy* grapes

Nothing shouts "Fri-yay!" like a sensational salami rose (see opposite); add crunch with fruit-and-nut crisps and Marcona almonds

(Fun fact: Marconas are known as the "queen of almonds" and are often paired with sherry, er, milk.)

Ham-wrapped grissini (thin, crispy breadsticks), green olives, and melon butterflies

(if you must have butterflies in your stomach, they might as well be of the cantaloupe and watermelon persuasion)

A VERY IMPRESSIVE SALAMI ROSE

1. Set a wineglass and a champagne flute on the table. Fill the wineglass halfway with ice. Add 1½ ounces Aperol, 3 ounces Prosecco, and a splash of club soda. Garnish with an orange slice. (In case you haven't guessed, this glass is for you.)
2. For the champagne flute, fold one slice of salami over the rim and layer slices one at a time on top, overlapping the previous slice by all but an inch, until you've worked your way around the flute at least once, several times for more petals.
3. Invert the flute into a lunchbox compartment. Remove the glass, leaving behind your very impressive salami rose.
4. Toast your success.

PITAPALOOZA

There are many marvelous things about mezze (a Mediterranean platter of dips, salads, and snacks), but its stability in warm climates—be it Greece, the Middle East, or a school locker—makes it particularly perfect for the lunchbox. This also means it's apt to stay fresh in the fridge throughout the school week, so you could prep everything on Sunday and just scoop/plop/place the components in the lunchbox compartments in a few minutes.

To mix up mezze for the lunchbox, we made our falafel a little easier (because it's baked, not fried), our Herby Olives DIY (because the olive bar adds up), and our Chocolate Pistachio Drops out of this world (because grown-ups need cookies, too). We also turned up the protein quotient of already healthful tabbouleh by adding quinoa, which you'll see once by its lonesome and once stuffed into a pita (which is a great way to make any grain salad easier

for kids to eat). If tabbouleh is too much of a push for a picky eater, the mini pita in Day 2: Pocket Luncher can also be a nice vehicle for hummus, tomatoes, and cucumbers, or just one of those.

This brings us to another thing we love about mezze—these boxes are easy to customize. If you know, say, that one of your kids likes hummus while another prefers tzatziki, you can pack accordingly. While we're personalizing, we highly recommend finding a canned main option that your kid loves, be it dolmas, tuna, or chickpeas. On the days you seem to have run out of everything, it's nice to know there's a win waiting in the pantry.

Lastly, since we always seem to have a few pita wallowing in the bread box, we have a recipe for how to turn it into crackers of all shapes, including a (not) terrifying pitasaurus to surprise and delight on Fri-yay.

WEEK 5

DAY 1	DAY 2	DAY 3	DAY 4	DAY 5
Mediterranean Monday	Pocket Luncher	Take Another Little Pita My Heart	Falafel Shuffle	Pitasaurus Box

MEAL PREP

SUNDAY

Bake the **Pita Punchies** (page 154).
Mix up a batch of **Herby Olives** (page 154).
Make the **Chocolate Pistachio Drops** (page 156); definitely have your kitchen helpers assist with the chocolate dip.
Prep the **Tasty Tabbouleh** (page 155).

MONDAY

If you ate all the **Tasty Tabbouleh** (it happens), make another batch.
Make the **Spinach Hummus** (page 52), or you can opt for any flavor of a store-bought brand.

TUESDAY

Pit the cherries if your child is little, or favors food fights.

WEDNESDAY

Make the **Lemony Tahini Yogurt Dip** (page 59).
Make the **Baked Falafel** (page 157).

THURSDAY

Finish off the rest of the **Chocolate Pistachio Drops** and get excited about tomorrow's Jurassic Parsley extravaganza!

GROUP PROJECT: Kids could certainly help with the Pita Punchies, but since it's more fun to be surprised by T. rex crackers, we suggest distracting them with the Chocolate Pistachio Drops; the sooner they learn how to make these for you, the better.

SHOPPING LIST

MEAT + DELI

- [ ] 1 cup brine-cured green and black olives

DAIRY CASE

- [ ] 1 stick unsalted butter
- [ ] 1 block of feta
- [ ] Plain full-fat Greek-style yogurt (you'll need ¼ cup)

PRODUCE

- [ ] 3 lemons
- [ ] 2 tangerines
- [ ] ¼ cup pomegranate seeds
- [ ] ½ pound cherries
- [ ] 2 apricots
- [ ] 3 Persian cucumbers
- [ ] 1 pint cherry tomatoes
- [ ] 1 small yellow onion
- [ ] 1 bunch scallions

- [ ] 1 (5-ounce) bag spinach
- [ ] 1 head of garlic
- [ ] 1 bunch fresh curly parsley
- [ ] 1 bunch fresh mint
- [ ] 1 bunch fresh cilantro

BREAD + SNACK FOODS

- [ ] 1 package pita breads
- [ ] 1 package mini pita breads (optional)
- [ ] 1 box sweet potato crackers

PANTRY + BULK

- [ ] 1 can dolmas
- [ ] 1 bag dried apricots
- [ ] 1 chocolate bar
- [ ] ¼ pound almonds
- [ ] ¼ pound roasted pistachios
- [ ] ⅓ cup dried quinoa

- [ ] ½ cup dark or milk chocolate chips
- [ ] 1 (15.5-ounce) can chickpeas
- [ ] Tahini
- [ ] 1 cup dried chickpeas
- [ ] Extra-virgin olive oil
- [ ] Kosher salt and black pepper
- [ ] Ground coriander
- [ ] Ground cumin
- [ ] Paprika
- [ ] Ground cinnamon
- [ ] All-purpose flour
- [ ] Chickpea flour
- [ ] Baking soda
- [ ] Confectioners' sugar
- [ ] Pure vanilla extract
- [ ] Dried (or fresh) rosemary, thyme, and/or oregano

EXTRA

- [ ] Gummy bears (optional, but sure to be loved)

CHEAT SHEET: Stop by your favorite prepared-foods case to stock up for this week if you're not in the mood to cook. Buy 1 cup olives, pita chips, a pint of tabbouleh from the deli case, one container of spinach hummus, six falafel, premade tahini sauce or tzatziki, and a box of store-bought cookies. Make sure you update your shopping list if you choose to swap a store-bought ingredient for a homemade item.

WEEK 5 *Recipes*

PITA PUNCHIES   MAKES ABOUT TWELVE 3-INCH CRACKERS OR NINETY-SIX 1-INCH CRACKERS

4 regular (not mini) pita breads,
  about 8 inches in diameter
Extra-virgin olive oil
Kosher or sea salt

1. Preheat the oven to 350°F. Line a sheet pan with parchment paper.
2. Use cookie cutters of your choice to punch shapes out of the pita breads (we like a mix of 3-inch and 1-inch shapes). Brush both sides of each shape with the oil and sprinkle with salt. Bake for 12 to 15 minutes, flipping everything over halfway through, until golden and crispy. (You can also bake the scraps alongside; they aren't as cute, but they're just as tasty.) Let cool completely on the sheet pan, pack in the lunchbox, and store extras in an airtight container for up to 5 days.

HERBY OLIVES   MAKES ABOUT 1 CUP

1 cup mixed green and
  black brine-cured olives
1 tablespoon extra-virgin olive oil
1 teaspoon chopped fresh or dried
  rosemary, thyme, and/or oregano
¼ teaspoon grated tangerine zest
Pinch of kosher salt
Pinch of black pepper

Stir together the olives, oil, herbs, zest, salt and pepper in an airtight container. Store in the refrigerator for up to 1 week. (The oil will seize in the fridge, but a short rest inside a room-temperature lunchbox will render everything appetizing-looking again.)

TASTY TABBOULEH MAKES ABOUT 2 CUPS

⅓ cup dried quinoa

½ teaspoon grated lemon zest

2 tablespoons fresh lemon juice

1 garlic clove, grated

2 tablespoons extra-virgin olive oil

¼ teaspoon kosher salt

⅛ teaspoon black pepper

Pinch of ground cinnamon

½ cup finely chopped fresh curly
  parsley

½ cup cherry tomatoes, quartered

1 Persian cucumber, halved lengthwise
  and cut into ¼-inch-thick half circles
  (about ½ cup)

2 tablespoons finely chopped fresh
  mint

1 scallion, thinly sliced

Mini pita breads (optional)

1. Place the quinoa in a fine-mesh strainer, rinse well under cold running water, and drain. Stir together the quinoa, ⅔ cup water, and a big pinch of salt in a small saucepan. Bring to a boil over medium-high heat, reduce the heat to low, cover, and simmer until all the water has been absorbed, 10 to 12 minutes. Let rest with the lid on for 10 minutes, then fluff with a fork.

2. Whisk together the lemon zest, lemon juice, and garlic in a small bowl. Slowly whisk in the oil, then whisk in the salt, pepper, and cinnamon.

3. In a medium bowl, stir together the quinoa, parsley, cherry tomatoes, cucumber, mint, and scallion. Drizzle with the lemon dressing and gently toss to coat (or, for maximum freshness, hold the dressing until just before serving).

4. Transfer to a lunchbox compartment and pack utensils, or stuff inside a mini pita (if using) for easier eating. Store extras in an airtight container in the refrigerator for up to 3 days.

CHOCOLATE PISTACHIO DROPS MAKES 24

½ cup shelled roasted pistachios
  (about ¼ pound unshelled)

1 cup all-purpose flour

⅛ teaspoon kosher salt

½ cup (1 stick) unsalted butter,
  at room temperature

¼ cup confectioners' sugar

1 teaspoon pure vanilla extract

3 ounces (about ½ cup) dark or
  milk chocolate chips, melted

1. Preheat the oven to 350°F. Line a sheet pan with parchment paper.
2. Grind the pistachios in a food processor until finely chopped, 10 to 15 seconds. Reserve 2 tablespoons and set aside. Transfer the remaining pistachios to a small bowl and mix in the flour and salt. In the bowl of a stand mixer fitted with the paddle attachment, cream the butter, sugar, and vanilla on medium speed until smooth and creamy, about 1 minute. Add the pistachio-flour mixture and mix on low speed until the dough comes together.
3. Pinch off a piece of the dough, roll it into a ball about the size of a cherry tomato, and place it on the sheet pan. Continue until you have used all the dough, placing the balls 1½ inches apart; you should have about 24 balls. Bake until the tops are slightly crackly and the bottoms are lightly browned, 12 to 14 minutes. Remove the cookies from the oven and let cool completely on the sheet pan.
4. Dip the top of each cookie into the melted chocolate and immediately sprinkle with a pinch of the reserved pistachios. Let the cookies set for 15 minutes, then store in an airtight container at room temperature for up to 3 days. Pack in the lunchbox right before school.

BAKED FALAFEL MAKES 12

1 cup dried chickpeas (canned
   chickpeas will turn to mush)

½ small yellow onion, chopped

¾ cup packed fresh curly parsley

¾ cup packed fresh cilantro

2 large garlic cloves

2 teaspoons ground cumin

1 teaspoon ground coriander

1 teaspoon kosher salt

½ teaspoon black pepper

½ teaspoon baking soda

¼ cup chickpea flour

1. Soak the chickpeas overnight, or quick-soak them (see Tiny Tip).
2. Position a rack in the center of the oven and preheat the oven to 375°F. Line a sheet pan with parchment paper.
3. Drain the chickpeas and pulse in a food processor until coarsely ground. Scrape into a bowl and set aside. To the bowl of the food processor (no need to wash), add the onion, parsley, cilantro, garlic, cumin, coriander, salt, pepper, and baking soda and process until fully combined into a finely minced paste. Return the chickpeas to the food processor, add the flour, and pulse to fully combine.
4. Use your hands to form the mixture into walnut-size balls or flatten into patties on the prepared pan, making 12 in all. (Heads up: To go full Falafel Shuffle on Thursday and Jurassic Parsley on Fri-yay you'll need to make both shapes.) Bake for 20 to 25 minutes, flipping midway through the cooking time (patties will cook more quickly than balls). Let cool and pack in the lunchbox or store in an airtight container in the refrigerator. The falafel are best eaten within 3 days, so plan to serve them on back-to-back days.

TINY TIP: To quick-soak chickpeas, cover with several inches of water in a medium pot, bring to a boil over high heat for 1 minute, remove from the heat, and set aside for 1 hour before draining.

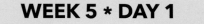

MEDITERRANEAN MONDAY

Bite-size homemade pita crackers, feta cubes, and a quinoa tabbouleh make for a very merry Monday mezze platter, lunchbox-style.

Herby Olives (page 154) + feta cubes with a curly parsley garnish

(if you have a soft spot for a classic curly parsley garnish, just wait until Fri-yay)

P.S. Got an olive avoider? Try raisins.

Crispy crunchy Pita Punchies (page 154)

a.k.a. the best possible use for stale pita breads

One lone **Chocolate Pistachio Drop** (page 156); it's quite possible you ate all the others already

Tasty **Tabbouleh (page 155)**

Don't forget to pack utensils; while tabbouleh *can* be eaten with one's fingers, there's a much higher likelihood of it ending up in your hair and behind your ears if you do.

Tangerine segments + pomegranate seeds

(Berry weird fact: Pomegranates are botanically classified as berries; but strawberries, raspberries, and blackberries aren't.)

POCKET LUNCHER

While completely ineffective as oven mitts or slippers, mini pita pockets *can* serve as fun and fetching leftover tabbouleh holders.

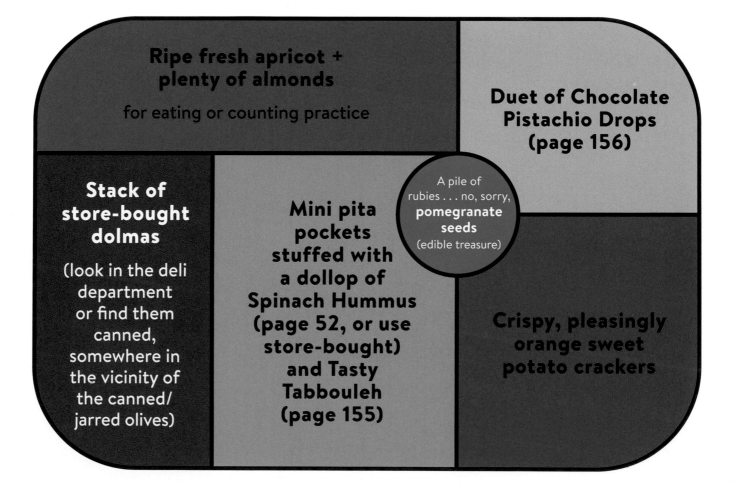

Ripe fresh apricot +
plenty of almonds

for eating or counting practice

Duet of Chocolate
Pistachio Drops
(page 156)

**Stack of
store-bought
dolmas**

(look in the deli
department
or find them
canned,
somewhere in
the vicinity of
the canned/
jarred olives)

**Mini pita
pockets
stuffed with
a dollop of
Spinach Hummus
(page 52, or use
store-bought)
and Tasty
Tabbouleh
(page 155)**

A pile of
rubies . . . no, sorry,
**pomegranate
seeds**
(edible treasure)

Crispy, pleasingly
orange sweet
potato crackers

TAKE ANOTHER LITTLE PITA MY HEART

Obviously this lunchbox title is even punnier if you have a 3-inch heart-shaped pita-punchie-maker, but we only had a bear.

Hearty handful of sweet little red cherries

Dark chocolate! Crunchy almonds! Sweet apricots!

What *isn't* hiding in this compartment?!

(A Pokémon . . . sorry)

Trio of store-bought dolmas

(see yesterday's note on sourcing)

Stack of bear-shaped *Pita Punchies* (page 154) for hummus dipping

An **Herby Olive** (page 154) center

Swirl of Spinach Hummus (page 52, or store-bought)

If your kiddo won't touch a swirl of green anything with a 10-foot pogo stick, just make/buy the regular kind.

FALAFEL SHUFFLE

Homemade falafel pack a lot of protein in herbaceous little packages. Admittedly, they can be a bit dry on their own, so be sure to include some hummus or tzatziki for dipping, or whip up the quick Lemony Tahini Yogurt Dip.

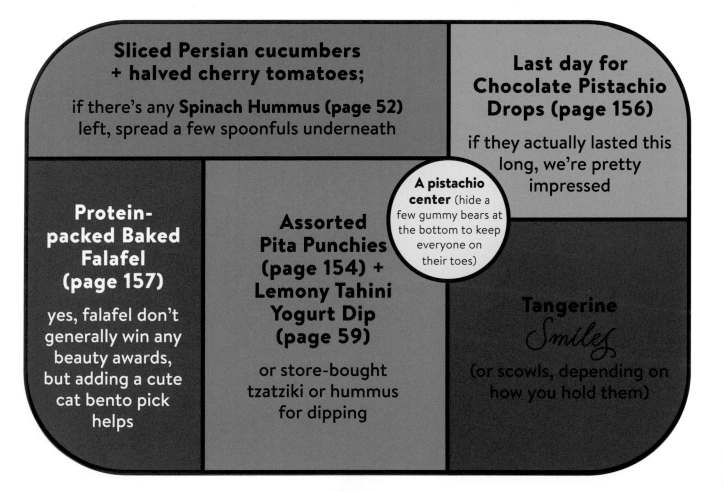

Sliced Persian cucumbers + halved cherry tomatoes;

if there's any **Spinach Hummus (page 52)** left, spread a few spoonfuls underneath

Last day for Chocolate Pistachio Drops (page 156)

if they actually lasted this long, we're pretty impressed

A pistachio center (hide a few gummy bears at the bottom to keep everyone on their toes)

Protein-packed Baked Falafel (page 157)

yes, falafel don't generally win any beauty awards, but adding a cute cat bento pick helps

Assorted Pita Punchies (page 154) + Lemony Tahini Yogurt Dip (page 59)

or store-bought tzatziki or hummus for dipping

Tangerine *Smiles*

(or scowls, depending on how you hold them)

PITASAURUS BOX

If you were wondering what to do with the leftover curly parsley from making Tasty Tabbouleh (page 155), wonder no more—it's a Jurassic Parsley kinda Fri-yay.

You've got pita bread, you've got a dinosaur cookie cutter, you've got a recipe for Pita Punchies (page 154)— how can you resist?

(We couldn't.) Just add a few falafel "rocks" (page 157), a cup of Lemony Tahini Yogurt Dip (page 59) or store-bought tzatziki or hummus for dipping, and a handful of Jurassic Parsley.

(In case you're wondering how we got that cucumber bone to float in the dip, it may or may not have involved a submerged cherry tomato half.)

Fresh ripe apricot + juicy little red cherries

Feta cubes + halved cherry tomatoes + Persian cucumber bones

(yes, there should be a wee 1-inch bone in that set of assorted food cutters that you now keep with you at all times)

SECRET GARDEN

Loading your little spinach skeptic's lunches with fruits and vegetables in disguise . . . devious or ingenious? You decide, but it's pretty clear which side we're on this week: Team CIA (Clandestine Incorporation of Avocado). Admittedly, adults are less-than-stellar secret agents when introducing veg-forward food to kids—either overselling it, inadvertently signaling anticipated rejection (and we all know kids can smell fear), or not even offering it, so certain they are of failure. This menu plan takes parents (and all possibility of self-sabotage) out of the mission by sending lunchboxes into the field.

At some point (how 'bout now?) we should warn you that this menu plan requires the most active cooking, so it would be perfectly reasonable (and maybe even advised, but who are we to limit you?) to choose just one lunchbox to make, and/or to make lunchboxes for dinner. All the lunches are packed with the good stuff parents love to push, but kids will be too busy cheering for their favorite foods to think anything of it. From the wondrous waffle and party-perfect chips with fresh salsa to both burrito bowl and burrito (because kids *really* like burritos) and, of course, pizza, we've got all the big hitters. Not to mention veggies in the form of popular sides, like chips and pickles.

Unquestionably, kids and veggies have one major thing in common: they both live for condiments. For this reason, we've included a dip for every main this week (well, aside from the main that *is* a dip, Cowpoke Caviar). We also used color to make each lunchbox pop, mostly through our Quickly Picklies, which are the prettiest preserved veg in the land thanks to stunning purple cauliflower. All together, we wanted each of these lunchboxes to look and feel like a party. Hopefully it's the celebration you'll be throwing yourself when your kid realizes they actually like vegetables.

WEEK 6

DAY 1	DAY 2	DAY 3	DAY 4	DAY 5
Waffle-y Good	Bean Me Up	Bowled Over	Neato Burrito	Double Dipping

MEAL PREP

SUNDAY

Make and freeze the **Carrot-Zucchini Chickpea Waffles** (page 172); toast them to reheat before packing the lunchbox.
Make a batch of **Quickly Picklies** (page 172).
Practice your kiwi-flower-carving skills (see page 177).

MONDAY

Make the **Cowpoke Caviar** (page 173).
Make the **Broccoli and Ricotta Bites** (page 174).

TUESDAY

Cook the brown rice and black beans (if DIYing versus using canned beans).

Bake the **Tahini Granola Bars** (page 175).
Mix the **Cilantro Avocado Dip** (page 58).

WEDNESDAY

Make the **Banana Freezer Cookies** (page 174).

THURSDAY

Mix the **Dilly Dip** (page 58) and **Hide 'n' Seek Red Sauce** (page 173).
Assemble and bake the **Pizza Rolls** (page 175).
Eat the rest of the mini dark chocolate nut butter cups after everyone goes to bed. You earned them.

GROUP PROJECT: Even the sous chef with the shortest attention span will be able to focus all the way through the Banana Freezer Cookies, which are also a great choice for kids who want to cook independently, since they require no baking.

SHOPPING LIST

DAIRY CASE
- [ ] Eggs (you'll need 4)
- [ ] 2 cheese squares or sticks
- [ ] 1 (8-ounce) block Colby
- [ ] ½ cup whole-milk ricotta
- [ ] ¾ cup plain yogurt
- [ ] Whole-milk mozzarella
- [ ] Unsalted butter

PRODUCE
- [ ] 1 nectarine
- [ ] 1 apricot
- [ ] 1 bunch grapes
- [ ] 2 kiwis
- [ ] ¼ cup pomegranate seeds
- [ ] 2 large limes
- [ ] 1 very ripe banana
- [ ] 1 lemon
- [ ] 1 handful fresh spinach
- [ ] 5 large carrots
- [ ] 1 zucchini
- [ ] ¼ pound green beans
- [ ] 1 orange sweet potato
- [ ] 1 avocado
- [ ] 1 bunch scallions
- [ ] 1 head cauliflower

- [ ] 1 head broccoli
- [ ] 1 head of garlic
- [ ] 3 Roma tomatoes
- [ ] 3 ears corn
- [ ] 2 red or orange bell peppers
- [ ] 1 small red onion
- [ ] 1 small butternut squash
- [ ] 1 bunch fresh cilantro
- [ ] 1 bunch fresh dill

BREAD + SNACK FOODS
- [ ] Mushroom chips
- [ ] Tortilla chips
- [ ] Vegetable chips
- [ ] 1 pound whole-wheat pizza dough
- [ ] Tortilla of choice

PANTRY + BULK
- [ ] 2 (15-ounce) cans black beans
- [ ] 1 (15-ounce) can black-eyed peas
- [ ] 1 (15-ounce) jar roasted red pepper slices
- [ ] Handful of black olives
- [ ] 1 teaspoon black peppercorns
- [ ] 1 cup chickpea flour
- [ ] ¾ cup mini chocolate chips

- [ ] Nutritional yeast
- [ ] 1 box crispy brown rice cereal
- [ ] ½ cup shredded coconut
- [ ] 1 (28-ounce) can whole peeled tomatoes
- [ ] White wine vinegar
- [ ] Brown rice
- [ ] Black olives
- [ ] Honey
- [ ] Baking powder
- [ ] Kosher salt and black pepper
- [ ] Garlic salt
- [ ] Extra-virgin olive oil
- [ ] Neutral oil, such as safflower
- [ ] Pure vanilla extract
- [ ] Quick-cooking and rolled oats
- [ ] Almond butter
- [ ] All-purpose flour
- [ ] Granulated sugar
- [ ] Dijon mustard
- [ ] Coconut oil
- [ ] Tahini
- [ ] Light agave nectar

EXTRA
- [ ] 1 bag miniature chocolate nut butter cups

CHEAT SHEET: If you prefer to buy dips instead of making your own, pick up a bottle of ranch and/or (for variety) green goddess dressing.

WEEK 6 *Recipes*

CARROT-ZUCCHINI CHICKPEA WAFFLES MAKES ABOUT EIGHT 4-INCH WAFFLES

½ cup grated carrot
½ cup grated zucchini
¼ cup thinly sliced
  scallions
2 tablespoons finely
  chopped fresh dill
1 cup chickpea flour

½ teaspoon kosher salt
1 teaspoon baking powder
½ cup water
2 large eggs
3 tablespoons neutral
  oil, such as avocado or
  grapeseed

Mix the carrot, zucchini, scallions, and dill in a small bowl. In a large bowl, whisk together the flour, salt, and baking powder, followed by the water, eggs, and oil. Add the carrot-zucchini mixture and mix well. Cook the waffles until crisp and golden (the exact cooking time will depend on your waffle maker). Store any extras in an airtight container in the freezer; pop them in the toaster for a few minutes before serving or packing in the lunchbox.

QUICKLY PICKLIES MAKES 1 PINT

¼ pound small thin green
  beans, ends trimmed
1 large carrot, sliced
  diagonally with a crinkle
  cutter or cut into sticks
4 dill sprigs
1 large garlic clove, sliced

½ cup white wine vinegar
½ cup water
1 tablespoon honey
1 tablespoon kosher salt
1 teaspoon black
  peppercorns

Pack the green beans, carrot, dill, and garlic into a wide-mouthed pint jar, such as a mason jar. Bring the vinegar, water, honey, salt, and peppercorns to a boil in a small saucepan over medium-high heat. Swirl until the honey and salt are dissolved, then pour over the vegetables until completely submerged. Let cool to room temperature, seal the jar with its lid, and refrigerate for up to 1 month.

COWPOKE CAVIAR MAKES ABOUT 2 QUARTS

Dressing
2 tablespoons extra-virgin olive oil
2 tablespoons fresh lime juice
1 tablespoon white wine vinegar
1 tablespoon honey
½ teaspoon kosher salt
½ teaspoon black pepper

Salad
1 (15-ounce) can black beans, rinsed
1 (15-ounce) can black-eyed peas, rinsed
3 Roma tomatoes, cored, seeded, and small diced (2 cups)
1 cup cooked fresh corn kernels, cut off steamed cobs
2 tablespoons minced red onion
1 cup small diced orange or red bell peppers
1 tablespoon seeded and minced jalapeño (optional)
Tortilla chips (optional)

1. To make the dressing: Whisk together the oil, lime juice, vinegar, honey, salt, and pepper in a small bowl.
2. To make the salad: Combine the black beans, black-eyed peas, tomatoes, corn, red onion, bell pepper, and jalapeño (if using) in a medium bowl. Drizzle the dressing over the salad and mix well. Store in an airtight container in the fridge for up to 1 week.
3. To serve, transfer to a leakproof lunchbox compartment or a lidded container. Pack with a spoon or tortilla chips, if desired, or tuck inside a quesadilla.

HIDE 'N' SEEK RED SAUCE MAKES ABOUT 6 CUPS

1 cup cubed peeled butternut squash (about 6 ounces)
2 large carrots, chopped into 2-inch segments (about 6 ounces)
1 garlic clove

1 (28-ounce) can whole peeled tomatoes
2 tablespoons extra-virgin olive oil
2 teaspoons sugar
1½ teaspoons kosher salt

Combine the squash, carrots, and garlic in a steamer basket set inside a pot with 1 inch of water. Bring to a boil over medium heat and steam until easily pierced with a fork, about 8 minutes. Carefully remove the basket and pour into a blender, along with the tomatoes, oil, sugar, and salt. Process until smooth. Refrigerate in an airtight container for up to 5 days.

BANANA FREEZER COOKIES MAKES 18

1 very ripe banana
1 teaspoon pure vanilla
  extract
1 cup quick-cooking oats

¼ cup almond butter
1 tablespoon honey
½ cup mini chocolate chips

1. Line a sheet pan with parchment paper, then call your kids to the kitchen because this recipe is just right for their attention span.
2. Combine the banana and vanilla in a medium bowl and mash with a fork until well-incorporated. Stir in the oats, almond butter, honey, and chocolate chips.
3. Roll into walnut-size balls and transfer to the sheet pan. Put the sheet pan in the freezer for 30 minutes to set (if desired, use a fork to smush into rounds at the 15-minute mark). Transfer the bites to a freezer bag or airtight container and freeze for up to 2 weeks. Pop them into the lunchbox in the morning. (Bites will be thawed or chilled, but not frozen, by lunchtime.)

BROCCOLI AND RICOTTA BITES SERVES 2

¼ cup whole-milk ricotta
¼ cup plain yogurt
2 tablespoons unsalted
  butter, melted and
  cooled
1 large egg
¼ cup all-purpose flour
½ teaspoon baking powder
½ teaspoon kosher salt

¼ cup finely chopped
  broccoli or cauliflower
  florets
2 tablespoons chopped
  fresh dill or basil
2 tablespoons neutral oil,
  such as safflower or
  vegetable oil

1. Dig out your cookie cutters and find a shape that will fit in the lunchbox compartment. Line a plate with a paper towel.
2. Whisk together the ricotta, yogurt, butter, and egg in a medium bowl until smooth. In a small bowl, stir together the flour, baking powder, salt, and pepper until combined, then add to the ricotta mixture and whisk until combined. Stir in the broccoli and dill.
3. Heat 1 tablespoon of the oil in a nonstick skillet over medium heat and swirl in the pan to coat. Working in batches, drop the batter by tablespoon (or more, if you've chosen a larger cutter) into the pan. Cook for about 2 minutes on each side. Transfer to the prepared plate. Cool, cut each into the desired shape, and transfer to the lunchbox. Serve the same day.

TAHINI GRANOLA BARS MAKES 12 BARS

1½ cups rolled oats (or quick-cooking oats for pickier eaters)

¾ cup crispy brown rice cereal

½ cup unsweetened shredded coconut

¼ cup mini chocolate chips

½ teaspoon kosher salt

1 large egg white

½ cup tahini

¼ cup light agave nectar

2 tablespoons coconut oil, melted

1 teaspoon pure vanilla extract

1. Position a rack in the center of the oven and preheat the oven to 325°F. Line a 9-inch square baking pan with a parchment paper sling.
2. Stir together the oats, rice cereal, coconut, chocolate chips, and salt in a large bowl. In a medium bowl, whisk the egg white until frothy, then whisk in the tahini, agave, oil, and vanilla until fully combined. Pour over the oat mixture and mix well.
3. Press into the prepared pan with clean hands or a silicone spatula. Bake for 20 to 25 minutes, until the oats turn golden. Let cool in the pan for 1 hour. Transfer to a cutting board and slice into 12 bars or 36 (1½-inch) bites (a nice size for younger kids especially). Store in an airtight container for up to 1 week.

PIZZA ROLLS MAKES 12 ROLLS

1 pound store-bought whole-wheat pizza dough

¼ cup Hide 'n' Seek Red Sauce (page 173) or store-bought marinara

¼ cup jarred roasted red pepper slices, drained and patted dry

¾ cup shredded whole-milk mozzarella

Garlic salt

1. Preheat the oven to 425°F. Line a sheet pan with parchment paper for easier cleanup.
2. Roll the pizza dough into a roughly 9-by-12-inch rectangle. Spread the red sauce in a thin layer over the dough, leaving a 1-inch border. Arrange the red pepper slices evenly on top and sprinkle with the mozzarella.
3. Starting from one long side, roll the dough tightly into a cylinder. Place the cylinder seam-side down on the counter and let rest for 15 minutes, then slice it into 1-inch-wide segments. Arrange them face-up on the sheet pan (think: cinnamon rolls) and sprinkle with garlic salt. Bake for 15 minutes, then let cool.
4. Transfer to the lunchbox, or store in an airtight container at room temperature for up to 3 days.

WAFFLE-Y GOOD

Hide a few handfuls of shredded carrot and zucchini in these savory gluten-free waffles, then see if your cauliflower-resistant luncher will cave if said crucifer is the same color as Share Bear.

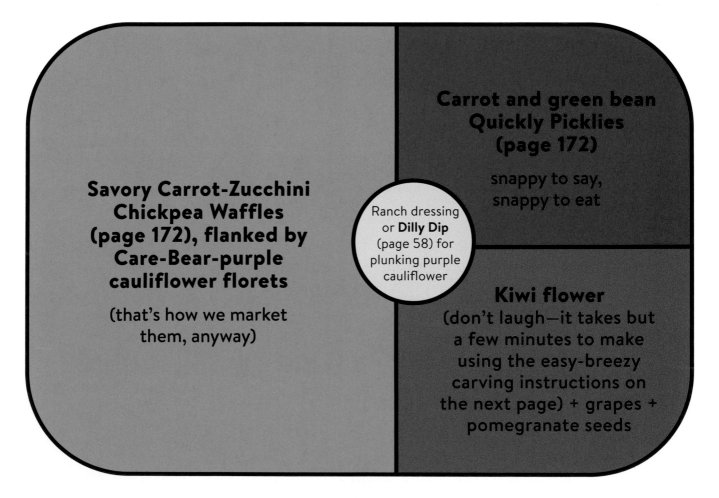

Savory Carrot-Zucchini Chickpea Waffles (page 172), flanked by Care-Bear-purple cauliflower florets

(that's how we market them, anyway)

Ranch dressing or **Dilly Dip** (page 58) for plunking purple cauliflower

Carrot and green bean Quickly Picklies (page 172)

snappy to say, snappy to eat

Kiwi flower (don't laugh—it takes but a few minutes to make using the easy-breezy carving instructions on the next page) + grapes + pomegranate seeds

FRUIT FLOWER POWER

With 5 minutes and a few satisfying stabs of a paring knife, you can add "expert kiwi carver" to your résumé (this technique also works for the grape flowers on page 212).

If your efforts are less than successful, eat the mangled kiwi, google "kiwi flower carving YouTube," and try, try again.

1. Using your sharpest paring knife, carefully trim all the skin off the kiwi.
2. Turn the kiwi on its side and use the tip of the knife to make a ½-inch-long angled cut through its equator, slicing at least halfway through the fruit. Continue circling the kiwi's equator, making a parallel cut every ½ inch, then reverse direction and make cuts going the other way (imagine you're tracing a zigzag pattern around the kiwi with the knife).
3. Gently pry the halves apart. If any of the "petals" stick, carefully cut them free.

BEAN ME UP

Covert broccoli is the star of this box (quite literally). Mushrooms masquerade in crispy crunchy chip form, and vegetable-packed Cowpoke Caviar beckons seed-packed chips.

Crispy Crunchy Champignon Mushroom Snack

It's a superfood fungus, it's a chip, it's . . . both?

Sweet, ripe summer nectarine

almost universally popular, so probably no need for a mustache and glasses disguise

Broccoli and Ricotta Bites (page 174)

cut into stars or hearts or honey badgers—whatever cookie cutter you've got

Hard to resist the siren call of keenly **crispy chia and quinoa chips** (we like Late July brand); you can of course use regular tortilla chips instead

Round up a cup of fancy *Cowpoke Caviar* (page 173), plus a couple of snack-size pieces of Cheddar

10 TANTALIZING SNACKS

When we grilled our grocers about their under-the-radar favorite snack, mushroom chips (shown below) were their hot tip. We also love . . .

1. Dehydrated strawberries
2. Rice cracker mix
3. Trail mix
4. Mini cheese sandwich crackers
5. Pea crisps
6. Peanut butter puffs
7. Individual-serving guacamole
8. Roasted seaweed
9. Cheese sticks or Babybel
10. Tea cakes (and, really, all mini desserts)

BOWLED OVER

Technically, this rice bowl is a box, but you know what we mean. Also, studies (or very loosely administered nonscientific polls) show that vegetables are more desirable when arranged diagonally.

Shredded Colby (two colors in one cheese = strange magic) **+ Cilantro Avocado Dip (page 58)** (or store-bought Green Goddess dressing)

Tahini Granola Bars (page 175) cut into squares (or stars or crumbles— all are delicious)

Pomegranate **seeds** (in related news, today is a good day for a navy or black T-shirt)

Snappy snack that suspiciously resembles vegetables but tastes like chips (i.e., veggie chips from the bulk bins)

Steamed sweet potato cubes, broccoli florets, brown rice sprinkled with nutritional yeast— a.k.a. nooch (now try to stop saying "nooch" all day long . . . you're welcome)—and black beans

NEATO BURRITO

The thing that is extra neato about a burrito is that you can put pretty much anything you want in there (except, perhaps, pudding). Since this week of lunches is all about the power of plants, we opted to try to stuff in a summer garden's worth.

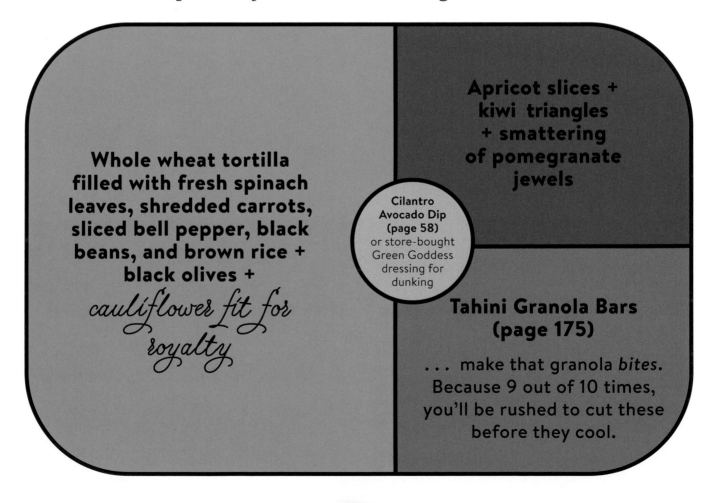

Whole wheat tortilla filled with fresh spinach leaves, shredded carrots, sliced bell pepper, black beans, and brown rice + black olives +

cauliflower fit for royalty

Cilantro Avocado Dip (page 58) or store-bought Green Goddess dressing for dunking

Apricot slices + kiwi triangles + smattering of pomegranate jewels

Tahini Granola Bars (page 175)

. . . make that granola *bites*. Because 9 out of 10 times, you'll be rushed to cut these before they cool.

DOUBLE DIPPING

Just when you thought pizza couldn't get any more exciting, today's Fri-yay surprise is pizza . . . *rolls*. Kids can't resist them, lunchbox preppers can hide vegetables in their sauce, everyone wins.

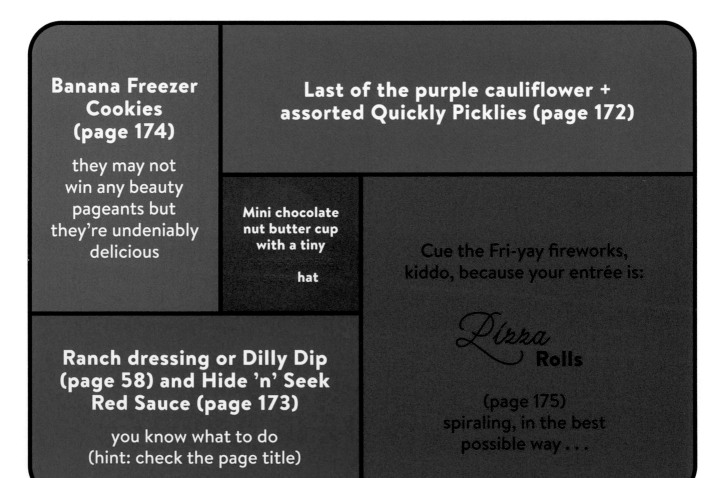

Banana Freezer Cookies (page 174)

they may not win any beauty pageants but they're undeniably delicious

Last of the purple cauliflower + assorted Quickly Picklies (page 172)

Mini chocolate nut butter cup with a tiny hat

Ranch dressing or Dilly Dip (page 58) and Hide 'n' Seek Red Sauce (page 173)

you know what to do (hint: check the page title)

Cue the Fri-yay fireworks, kiddo, because your entrée is:

Pizza **Rolls**

(page 175) spiraling, in the best possible way . . .

CHAPTER

4

KNOCK YOURSELF OUT

**LUNCH BOXERS,
ENTER THE RING**

When you're ready to make childhood memory gold, this is the chapter for you. Because while most days call for a nutritious, balanced, and (relatively) easy-to-pull-together lunchbox, other days call for the big W-O-W. In this chapter of very special lunchboxes, you'll find any number of ways to delight your little lunchers. (If you want to take a second to paper-clip the pages together to keep little eyes from spoiling their surprises, please do.) These lunchboxes are for holidays, birthdays, and the small but important days that mean a lot to the lunchbox set but can slip by adults—when kids have a loose tooth, or their favorite animal returns to the zoo, or they have a tea party playdate, or it's time to hop on an airplane to visit grandma.

While we love scrolling through the extraordinarily intricate bento and bento-inspired boxes on social media (people are amazing!), we hope they won't scare you off by setting an unrealistic bar. We can assure you that adult standards for food art greatness are considerably higher than children's, and besides, we're after more licks (as in, the lunchbox clean) than likes here. (Although if you post pictures of these lunches, you'll get those, too.) In this chapter, you'll find delectable designs that kids will want to eat (as well as look at), that contain enough food to count as a meal, and that you can actually make. In other words, impressive but not impossible. Because at the end of the day (and book), when we look at a lunchbox, we see an audience of two—the person making it and the person eating it—and we want you both to have the best time.

Ready for your final hurrah? Let's go.

FIRST DAY OF SCHOOL

Who has time for first-day-of-school jitters when
there are school bus sandwiches, cheese pencils,
and schoolboy cookies to be eaten?!

HOW TO BUILD A SCHOOL BUS SANDWICH

1. Place a slice of yellow Cheddar over a slice of bread, trim away any underhanging bread, and use a sharp paring knife to cut a gentle curve into the top two corners.
2. Cut a windshield out of a slice of white Cheddar, and bisect it vertically with a thin scrap of yellow Cheddar.
3. Slice small strips of raspberry or grape fruit leather to make the bumper, grill, and windshield wipers.
4. Find something small and round (button, hoop earring, M&M) and use it to trace and cut two headlights out of the white Cheddar scraps.
5. Cut one red and one yellow jelly bean in half to create signal lights above the windshield (M&M's work too; glue them down with a dab of honey).
6. Trim the holey end off of two black olives and turn them into wheels.
7. Cut another black olive in half lengthwise and nestle one half on each side of the bus; this creates rearview mirrors *and* helps hold the bus in place during its ride to school.

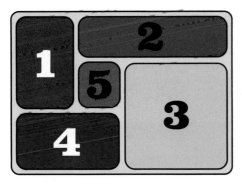

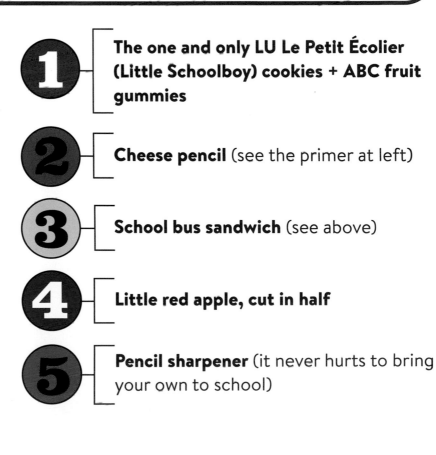

1 The one and only LU Le Petit Écolier (Little Schoolboy) cookies + ABC fruit gummies

2 **Cheese pencil** (see the primer at left)

3 **School bus sandwich** (see above)

4 **Little red apple, cut in half**

5 **Pencil sharpener** (it never hurts to bring your own to school)

CHEESE PENCIL PRIMER

BASE: Cheddar cheese stick

ERASER: Red apple

FERRULE: Foil (the metal band between the pencil wood and the eraser is called a ferrule; see, everyone is learning here)

TIP: White Cheddar triangle + black sesame seed (or a speck of black olive, fruit leather scrap, or burnt toast crumb)

FUN & GAMES

It's all fun and games until someone loses a watermelon die under the cafeteria table; thankfully, they've still got a tic-tac-toe pizza board to keep the lunch party going.

FROM ENGLISH MUFFIN TO MACGUFFIN

Turn an otherwise uninteresting English muffin into a real player in four easy steps.

1. Split the muffin and slather each half with whatever red sauce is in your fridge. (We like Rao's; or DIY using the recipe on page 173.)
2. Sprinkle shredded mozzarella on top. Place four ¼-inch-thick slices of bell pepper in a grid to create a tic-tac-toe board.
3. Bake both halves in a toaster oven until satisfyingly melty and slightly toasted.
4. Use a 1-inch circle cutter and 1-inch letter X cutter to stamp out at least four turkey pepperoni Xs and Os. Arrange them on the board in a cunning opening move, or next to the pizza, to invite a game of tic-tac-toe before lunch. (If you cut extra letters, stack the pieces on top of each other, as seen here.)

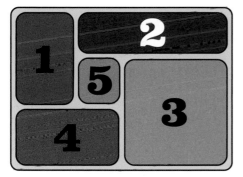

1 Checkerboard cookies + Chessmen cookies (Jovial Foods and Pepperidge Farm brand, respectively)

2 Watermelon dice with black sesame seed dots

3 English muffin pizza (see above)

4 Tangerine PAC-MAN + cucumber ghosts (carved with a sharp paring knife or X-Acto knife and decorated with candy eyeballs)

5 Scrabble tiles that spell "F-U-N" or your child's initials or their favorite three-letter Scrabble word

HALLOWEEN

Wish your little ghoul or ghost happy hauntings and send them on their merry scary way with this monstrously fun lunch.

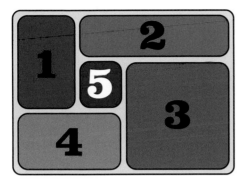

1 **Grape eyeballs** (lop the tops off a few green grapes, add candy eyeballs) **+ tangerine-o'-lanterns** (cut a tangerine in half, then use a sharp paring knife or X-Acto knife to carve a crooked grin into each rounded side)

2 **Cats and bats melon cutouts**

3 **Franken-burrito** (stuff a 10-inch spinach tortilla with your filling of choice, slice a pimento-stuffed green olive in half to make the eyes, and use scissors to cut a strip of roasted seaweed snack into hair, nose, and stitches)

Yes, this lunchbox is conspicuously candy-free, but since your bantam bogeyman will eat approximately 200 pounds of candy corn, Skittles, and miniature Milky Ways before the full moon rises, we think that makes spookily good sense.

4 **Green apple goblins** (cut an apple into quarters, cut a wedge out of the middle of each quarter to form a mouth, poke sunflower seeds into the top and bottom of the wedge to make teeth, and add candy eyeballs; strawberry slice tongue optional)

HEY, BOO: In case you didn't notice, this box is heavy on the candy eyeballs, that hallowed Halloween staple and general joy generator. You can make your own with royal icing, but they're easy enough to order online or track down at your local Target or craft store.

5 **Babybel cheese spider** (use a sharp paring knife or X-Acto knife to cut four long skinny strips on each side of the cheese round, then gently bend each leg into place and add candy eyeballs)

HAPPY BIRTHDAY

It's your little luncher's big day—help them get their sprinkle on.

THREE-LAYER BIRTHDAY SANDWICH LOGISTICS

1. Layer two slices of sandwich bread with mayonnaise, mustard, turkey, and yellow Cheddar (or use fillings of your choice). Trim the crusts and slice the sandwich horizontally into three equal strips.

2. Place one strip sideways in the lunchbox, so the layers are visible. Trim an inch or so off the sides of the two remaining strips and stack them sideways on top of the first, to create a three-layer effect.

3. Cut three ¼-by-2-inch strips of mini bell pepper and place them on top as "candles." Using small, sharp scissors or an X-Acto knife, cut or carve three tiny bell pepper "flames" and pop them on top of the candlesticks. (If your school is cool with it, you can substitute bona fide birthday candles.

4. Snack on the scraps as you fantasize about *your* perfect birthday lunch (poolside fish tacos and margaritas, probably).

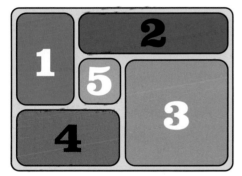

1 **Cantaloupe cutout flowers with green grape slice centers, matcha Pocky stick stems** (gently push the end of the Pocky stick into the melon to make it stick), **and mint leaves**

2 **pretzel twists dipped in melted dark chocolate and rolled in sprinkles**

3 **three-layer birthday sandwich** (see above) **with bell pepper candles**

4 **mini confetti cupcake cut in half**

5 **"gift-wrapped" candy** (Starburst are a natural for this project)

WIGGLY TOOTH

Loose tooth wiggling all about? This box will help you pull it out.
(And make sure you're fairly compensated for it, too.)

APPLE CRUMBLE BARS MAKES 9 SQUARE BARS

Filling
3 cups finely diced peeled apples (about 5 small apples)
½ cup granulated sugar
2 teaspoons cornstarch
2 teaspoons fresh lemon juice
1 teaspoon ground cinnamon
½ teaspoon pure vanilla extract
½ teaspoon kosher salt

Crust and Crumble
2 cups all-purpose flour
1 cup almond flour
¾ cup rolled oats
¾ cup cold unsalted butter, cubed
½ cup packed brown sugar
¾ teaspoon kosher salt
2 large eggs

1. Position a rack in the center of the oven and preheat the oven to 350°F. Butter a 9-inch square baking pan.
2. To make the filling: Combine the apples, sugar, cornstarch, lemon juice, cinnamon, vanilla, and salt in a large bowl and set aside.
3. To make the crust and crumble: Using a food processor, process the all-purpose flour, almond flour, oats, butter, brown sugar, and salt until crumbly. Add the eggs and pulse until the mixture begins to come together. Press three-quarters of the mixture into the bottom of the pan and top with filling, then sprinkle the remainder to cover.
4. Bake for 40 to 45 minutes, until the crumble is golden and the apples are soft. Cool completely, cut into bars, and store at room temperature in an airtight container for up to 3 days.

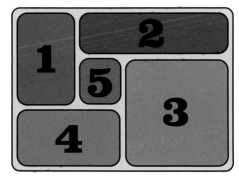

1 **Supplies for writing the tooth fairy + envelope** for safely storing the tooth

2 **Red and green apple slices + Babybel cheese-child** (see page 33), sans tooth

3 **Tooth-shaped cream cheese and raspberry jam sandwich on a bed of blueberries**

4 **Apple Crumble Bar** (see above; for those who prefer slow and gentle tooth removal) **+ caramel stick** (for those who don't)

5 **Crunchy corn** (for those who wish to trick the tooth fairy)

100*th* DAY OF SCHOOL

Celebrate this meritorious midwinter milestone in scrumptious centennial style by arranging your mini mathematician's favorite foods in groups of ten. For your next trick, lead a "100 Bottles of Kombucha on the Wall" sing-along all the way to school.

10 WAYS FOR KIDS TO CELEBRATE 100

1. String 100 Cheerios on a piece of yarn to make a fetching necklace/wearable abacus.
2. Do 10 toe touches, jumping jacks, lunges, scissor jumps, Superman stretches, planks, push-ups, sit-ups, cartwheels, and laps around the kitchen.
3. Draw an illustration of how you'll look when you're 100 years old, standing next to your rocket car.
4. Stack 100 pennies on top of each other in 100 seconds, then call the Guinness World Records people because you probably just set one.
5. Play: "If I had $100, I would buy . . ."
6. Make a painting using only 100 of your thumbprints (then ask your parents to sell it as an NFT to fund your college education/first car/summer camp).
7. Read *Miss Bindergarten Celebrates the 100th Day of Kindergarten*, then discuss which "wonderful, one-hundred-full thing" you'd bring to school if you were in her class.
8. Use exactly 100 Legos or Lincoln Logs to build your pet hamster a small but lovely house.
9. Put together a 100-piece puzzle.
10. Say 100 thank-yous for this awesome lunch!

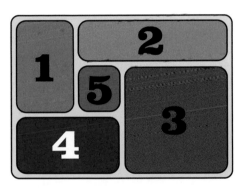

Here are 10 common kitchen items they can tally while you assemble this lunchbox:

1. Raisins
2. Cheerios
3. Pretzels
4. Dried beans
5. Popped popcorn kernels
6. Uncooked spaghetti noodles
7. Mom's/Dad's special beans (a.k.a. coffee beans)
8. Toast crumbs under the table
9. Mismatched Tupperware
10. Sesame seeds (in case 1–9 are too easy)

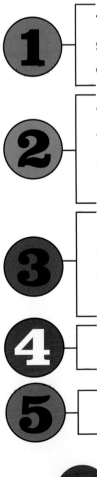

1 **10 crackers + plain yogurt for dipping salad components, etc. + apatosaurus cutout** (average life span: 100 years)

2 **10 Cheddar cubes + 100 cookies** (as in, they form the number 100, not 100 actual cookies, although that would likely be very well received)

3 **Deconstructed Waldorf salad—10 chicken cubes, 10 grapes, 10 apple cubes, 10 celery chunks, 10 walnuts, and 10 raisins or dried cranberries**

4 **10 cherries**

5 **10 jelly beans**

VALENTINE'S DAY

Nothing says "I love you" like stamping small hearts out of watermelon and painstakingly crafting tiny valentines out of cheese. But like we ask ourselves every February 14 at 5 a.m., WWCD (what would Cupid do)? This.

HOW TO PAINSTAKINGLY CRAFT TINY VALENTINES OUT OF CHEESE

Cut four 2½-by-2-inch slices of cheese—two white Cheddar, two yellow Cheddar. Stack one color on top of the other, cut a small triangle, and swap to create a different color "flap" for the "envelopes." Use a crinkle cut knife or scissors to cut three small "address" squiggles and a tiny "stamp" out of fruit leather. Should you have minuscule pink heart-shaped sprinkles sitting around the pantry (what do you know, we did!), use them to embellish the "stamp" and seal the envelope. Stack extra Cheddar scraps beneath the valentines, and congratulate yourself on this delightful artistic cheese feat! Or skip all that and just tuck a cute paper valentine in the box.

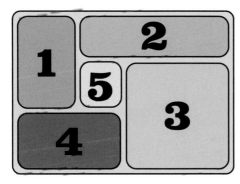

1 Cheddar valentines (see above)

2 Strawberry Pocky sticks + real live strawberry

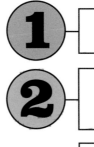

3 Heart-shaped waffles (we used a Dash mini heart waffle maker, but you can also just trim regular waffles with scissors) **garnished with a strawberry, cut into a heart and nestled in a bed of conversation hearts** (because this is the one day of the year when this seems perfectly permissible)

4 Heart-shaped watermelon cutouts

5 More conversation hearts (because they're only eating candy today and we all know it)

NOT-SO-LONELY HEARTS CLUB

Valentine's Day is fleeting, but leftover conversation hearts last forever. Here's how to repurpose your stockpile.

- Use them as game pieces (bingo board markers, Monopoly token stand-ins, poker chips)
- Glue them to a Popsicle stick frame, add a cute photo, and stick magnetic tape to the back, because you always need more fridge flair
- Grind them up in the food processor, stir in sugar and coconut oil, and voilà—instant body scrub

CAMPOUT

Pack the tent, s'mores sticks, bug spray, and this teeny-weenies-and-beanies-fortified snack set that's fit for either the wild and woolly wilderness or the lunchroom (same difference, really).

S'MORES SNACK MIX   MAKES ABOUT 1 CUP

½ cup honey grahams cereal (we like Mom's Best)

¼ cup mini marshmallows (don't skimp or you'll hear about it)

2 tablespoons chocolate chips (for you, and another for me ... just kidding, only 2 tablespoons)

Toss the ingredients together and serve, making a silent bet on how fast the marshmallows will disappear.

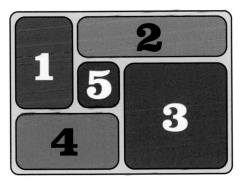

 Watermelon and cucumber butterfly cutouts (bears also work well; pair with a tutorial about campsite food lockers and the extreme importance of not storing snacks in your sleeping bag)

 S'mores Snack Mix (see above)

 Ritz cracker, peanut butter, pretzel stick, and mini sweet pepper "campfire" + miniature grass-fed beef weenies on pretzel sticks + cucumber tree cutouts

 Backup teeny weenies + baked beans

 Miniature compass to find your way back to the campsite/classroom

EARTH DAY

Honor Mother Earth by crafting her a definitely-not-to-scale portrait
on a rice cake, or a penne pasta necklace—every mom loves those—but
it'd have to be pretty long (as in 24,900 miles, or six trillion noodles).

CHERRY CHOCOCADO PUDDING MAKES ABOUT 3 CUPS

½ cup vanilla almond milk
2 tablespoons maple syrup
1 teaspoon pure vanilla
   extract
2 ripe medium avocados
   (nice and green inside,
   soft but still firm), pitted
   and peeled

1 (10-ounce) bag frozen
   dark sweet cherries
   (about 2 cups)
¼ cup unsweetened cocoa
   powder
1 tablespoon chia seeds
Pinch of ground cinnamon
Pinch of kosher salt

Combine all the ingredients in a high-speed blender or food processor and puree until very smooth. Taste for sweetness and add more maple syrup if desired. Serve immediately (cherry on top optional) or store in an airtight container in the refrigerator for up to 2 days.

MOTHER EARTH RICE CAKE HOW-TO

Slice a cucumber lengthwise with a vegetable peeler until you have roughly 10 thin slices, then layer them, overlapping slightly, on top of a rice cake spread with cream cheese, trying your best to construct some semblance of a continent using halved blueberries.

1 Steamed broccoli floret tree in a pretzel stick forest

2 Cherry tomato and blueberry ladybug skewers (cut two cherry tomatoes in half, slice them halfway down the center to create a split, skewer each one, adding half of a blueberry head as you go, then add black sesame seed spots, using a toothpick and honey to adhere, because you're dedicated like that)

3 Mother Earth rice cake

4 Cherry Chococado Pudding (see above) covered in chocolate cookie crumb "dirt" and a few strategically placed gummy worms

5 Cute pin, sticker, or other Earth Day–themed trinket

LET'S GO TO THE ZOO

Not school—the *other* zoo, the one with the lions, hippos, and panda bears, all of which are rendered edible in this ferociously fetching lunchbox.

SUSHI RICE MAKES ABOUT 2 CUPS

1 cup sushi rice (Japanese
   short-grain white rice)
2 tablespoons rice vinegar
1 tablespoon honey
½ teaspoon kosher salt

Cook the rice according to the directions on the package. When it's done, let it sit, covered, for 15 minutes. Bring the vinegar, honey, and salt nearly to a simmer in a small saucepan over medium-high heat, swirling until the honey and salt are completely dissolved. Place the rice in a large bowl, drizzle the vinegar mixture over, and gently fold it in with a spatula or rice paddle. Cover and let cool to room temperature. Use immediately for best results, or refrigerate overnight in an airtight container.

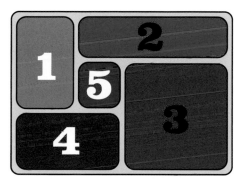

GUESS WHO'S GOBBLING WHAT?

Quiz your junior zookeeper on what they think the animals are eating for lunch, then reveal these answers.

ORANGUTANS: Lots of fruit

HIPPOS: Grass, leaves, fruit

PANDAS: Bamboo

RABBITS: Grass, hay, veggies

LIONS: Pretty much anything they can catch, but especially antelope, wildebeests, and zebras

1 **Banana chips** for your little monkey

2 **Celery log anchored by two Kinder Happy Hippo Cocoa Cream Biscuits,** because how do you resist

3 **PB+J pressed with a sandwich cutter, on a bed of julienned carrot shreds, with tangerine segment ears and neck, white Cheddar eyeballs and snout, chocolate chip pupils, blackberry nose, chive whiskers, and carrot tongue**

4 **Sushi Rice** (see above) **pressed in a panda rice ball mold** (available online) **and embellished with roasted seaweed trimmed using a cutter in that same kit**

5 **Neapolitan bunny grahams (Annie's brand)**

UP IN THE AIR

You won't hear a peep from the next seat once the lid goes up on this flying smorgasbord of snacks and distractibles. And yes, when the lid goes down, it's time to debut that new 199-episode animated series.

TRIO OF PLANE GAMES

Keep the kids entertained/not kicking the seat in front of them with these dandy diversions.

• Convert an extra lunchbox into a Lego kit, mini menagerie, or art supplies box.

• Try quiet time karaoke. Put on headphones and (silently!) sing along to your favorite song while the other player (who's also wearing headphones because no cheating) writes their best guess of the tune on a cocktail napkin. Dance moves encouraged.

• Request three unopened cans of pop, juice, and/or soda water from the flight attendant. Concoct interesting zero-proof cocktails and score the results (kid instructs; grown-up pours).

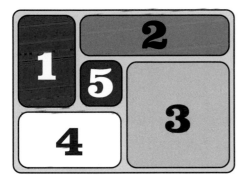

1 **Wind-up toy** (for tray table antics) **+ grapes + apple cutouts**

2 **Toy car + swap-a-point crayon pen + letter cookies subtly spelling F-L-Y**

3 **Apple and almond butter sandwich with white and yellow Cheddar cheese airplane and cloud cutouts** (optional but provide a mile-high delight factor)

4 **Tangerine + cloud cutout Pita Punchies** (page 154)

5 **A few Puntini Frutti jujube candies** (particularly pertinent if your final destination is Italy, Little Italy, or Rome, Georgia)

PARISIAN PICNIC

Just add a small striped shirt, scarf, and beret.
Bottle of Orangina and Eiffel Tower green screen optional.

LE FRENCH FOOD VOCABULARY

Teach your wee world traveler these helpful lunch-related phrases, so they're ready to hit the boulangerie or bistro at a moment's notice.

One baguette, please and thank you. // *Une baguette, s'il vous plaît et merci.*

Also three croissants. And a dozen madeleines. And an éclair. No, two. // *Aussi trois croissants. Et une douzaine de madeleines. Et un éclair. Non, deux.*

Please put extra ham and extra butter on my sandwich. // *S'il vous plaît, mettez du jambon et du beurre supplémentaires sur mon sandwich.*

This peach is so sweet. // *Cette pêche est si douce.*

I didn't get as many raspberries as my [sister/ brother/classmate/dog] did! // *Je n'ai pas eu autant de framboises que [ma soeur/mon frère/ ma camarade de classe/mon chien]!*

Did you know that you can eat the rind on Brie cheese? // *Saviez-vous que vous pouvez manger la croûte du fromage Brie?*

Only two macarons in my lunchbox? Is there a macaron shortage? // *Seulement deux macarons dans ma lunchbox? Y a-t-il une pénurie de macarons?*

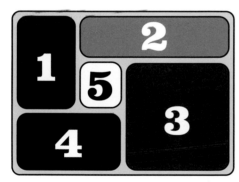

1 — **French Breakfast radishes and a wedge of Brie**

2 — **French-flag-patterned blueberries, white peaches, and red raspberries**

3 — **Ham and Gruyère sandwich on baguette** (gingham background optional but very on-theme)

4 — **Store-bought macarons**

5 — **Strawberry pâte de fruit**

TEA FOR TWO

A tantalizing tea box fit for royalty and portioned for you and a friend (real *or* imaginary; personally, we lean toward imaginary because we prefer not to share our curd).

MINI CITRUS SCONES MAKES 18

⅔ cup heavy cream, plus more for brushing

1 teaspoon pure vanilla extract

2 cups all-purpose flour, plus more for dusting

¼ cup sugar

2 teaspoons baking powder

½ teaspoon baking soda

¼ teaspoon kosher salt

1 tablespoon grated orange or lemon zest

½ cup (1 stick) cold unsalted butter, cubed

1. Line a rimmed sheet pan with parchment paper.
2. Stir together the cream and vanilla in a small bowl. In a food processor, pulse together the flour, sugar, baking powder, baking soda, salt, and zest. Add the butter and pulse until coarse crumbs form. Add the cream-vanilla mixture and pulse into a shaggy dough.
3. Turn the dough out onto a lightly floured surface and press it into a roughly 6-inch square. Cut the dough into thirds vertically. Cut each strip into three squares, then cut each square diagonally into two triangles. Place the scones on the sheet pan, with room to spread, and chill them in the refrigerator for 15 minutes.
4. Preheat the oven to 400°F. Brush the tops of the scones with heavy cream and bake for 10 to 12 minutes, until golden brown. Store in an airtight container at room temperature for up to 3 days.

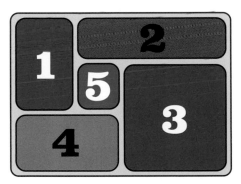

1 **Strawberries + Orange Curd** (page 79)

2 **Cucumber curls** (slice a cucumber end-to-end into thin strips with a vegetable peeler, curl, and skewer) **+ grape flowers** (see page 177)

3 Cucumber and Kerrygold butter tea sandwiches + strawberry and **Strawberry Cream Cheese** (page 53) sandwiches

4 **Mini Citrus Scones** (see above)

5 **Beautiful blushing rose** plucked from your or your green-thumbed neighbor's garden

SPACE CASE

It's Mars or bust for your little lunchonaut,
so build them a box that's truly out of this world.

SPACE CAMP

Before you blast off, here are some important things to know about infinity and beyond.

- It's more difficult to taste food in space, so remember to bring your hot sauce.

- Tortillas are OK in space, but bread is not, because without gravity, crumbs fly about endlessly.

- When astronauts have been asked to request their favorite foods for resupply, they've ordered macarons, kimchi, pizza, sushi, and fluffernutter sandwiches.

- M&M's are NASA's space candy of choice.

- Although developed by NASA, as of this writing, astronaut ice cream has never been eaten in space.

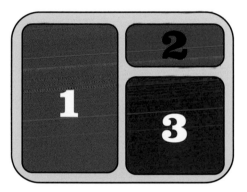

 Cheese sandwich rocket-powered by a carefully carved bell pepper booster + bell pepper galaxy not so far, far away

 Tangerine half-moons + blueberry black holes

 Extraterrestrial Babybel life (i.e., an excuse to use many, many candy eyeballs) + pretzel orbits

PARENTS' LUNCHBOX

As a parent, you wear many, many hats, not the smallest of which is Designated Scrap Scarfer. And so, this last box is for you, oh mighty carpool captain, homework helper, grocery gofer, wet swimsuit wrangler, road trip ringleader, bedtime boss, and so much more.

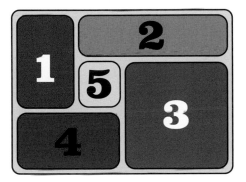

 1 Fruit and vegetable cutout scraps + cheese letter scraps

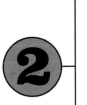 **2** Much-maligned egg yolks, rejected radish (sprinkled with Maldon salt, because you're worth it), **healthy granola bite that you stayed up late making and were so excited about but then you were flatly told by the recipient that they would "never in a million years" eat it**

 **3** Bear-shaped PB + J shadow scrap

 4 All the Goldfish cracker colors that did not meet muster for the Green Box (page 62) + broken bits left in the bottom of the bag after lunchbox pretzel twist distribution + really cool and interesting new Indian-inspired snack mix that was deemed way too spicy

 5 Mini cupcake with most of the frosting licked off, one bite taken, and no suspects in sight

FREAKY FRIDAY

It certainly doesn't maximize efficiency, and it may not have five-star results, but every so often, try asking your kids to make a lunchbox for you.

- Break out the kids' knives (we like Opinel's set) to prep fruit and veg together.

- Bring out bags of nuts and dried fruit so they can invent a trail mix.

- Set out the sandwich and lunchbox note supplies.

- Walk away.

- Will this be a boondoggle? A bridge to lunch-making independence?

- A lesson in gratitude? The best day of the dog's life? Who knows? You'll be too busy not making lunch to notice.

LUNCHLINE PUNCHLINE

Tucking a sweet note of encouragement into their lunchbox seemed like a great idea on the first day of school, but now it's day 118 and writer's block has hit. Don't fear, dad jokes are here. Jot down one of these tried and kid-tested food jokes for guaranteed laughs.

What did the mama olive say to the baby olive?
Olive you.

What does the Loch Ness monster eat for lunch?
Fish and ships.

What do you call a phony noodle?
An im-pasta.

What did the tortilla say when she saw the beans and cheese crying?
Wanna taco-bout it?

What do frogs eat for lunch?
French flies and pizzzzzza.

What do twins like to eat?
Pears.

Why do raspberries avoid rush hour traffic?
They don't want to get stuck in a jam.

What did the doctor say to the sick salami?
There's not much I can do, you're already cured.

What did the dumpling say to its dipping sauce?
I'm soy into you.

What did the rice cracker say to the peanuts?
You're nuts!

What did the baby fish say when his mom asked him to put away his toys?
Can't salmon else do it?

Where do butchers go to dance?
A meatball.

What do you call a sad cantaloupe?
Meloncholy.

Why was the mushroom the life of the party?
He was a fun-gi.

Why shouldn't you put more than 239 beans in your soup?
Just one more will make it two farty.

What did the hot cocoa say to the broken candy cane?
You look like you could use a little encourage-mint.

What kind of key can't open a lock?
A ki-wi.

Why did the garden feel safe?
Because all the vegetables knew carr-ate.

What do you call a peanut wearing a spacesuit?
An astro-nut.

How many varieties of olives grow on trees?
Olive them.

How do you make a burrito popular?
Stuff it with cool beans.

CONVERSION CHARTS

FRACTIONS	DECIMALS
⅛	.125
¼	.25
⅓	.33
⅜	.375
½	.5
⅝	.625
⅔	.67
¾	.75
⅞	.875

WEIGHTS

US/UK	METRIC
¼ oz	7 g
½ oz	15 g
1 oz	30 g
2 oz	55 g
3 oz	85 g
4 oz	110 g
5 oz	140 g
6 oz	170 g
7 oz	200 g
8 oz (½ lb)	225 g
9 oz	250 g
10 oz	280 g
11 oz	310 g
12 oz	340 g
13 oz	370 g
14 oz	400 g
15 oz	425 g
16 oz (1 lb)	455 g

VOLUME

AMERICAN	IMPERIAL	METRIC
¼ tsp		1.25 ml
½ tsp		2.5 ml
1 tsp		5 ml
½ Tbsp (1½ tsp)		7.5 ml
1 Tbsp (3 tsp)		15 ml
¼ cup (4 Tbsp)	2 fl oz	60 ml
⅓ cup (5 Tbsp)	2½ fl oz	75 ml
½ cup (8 Tbsp)	4 fl oz	125 ml
⅔ cup (10 Tbsp)	5 fl oz	150 ml
¾ cup (12 Tbsp)	6 fl oz	175 ml
1 cup (16 Tbsp)	8 fl oz	250 ml
1¼ cups	10 fl oz	300 ml
1½ cups	12 fl oz	350 ml
2 cups (1 pint)	16 fl oz	500 ml
2½ cups	20 fl oz (1 pint)	625 ml
5 cups	40 fl oz (1 qt)	1.25 l

OVEN TEMPERATURES

	°F	°C	GAS MARK
very cool	250–275	130–140	½–1
cool	300	148	2
warm	325	163	3
moderate	350	177	4
moderately hot	375–400	190–204	5–6
hot	425	218	7
very hot	450–475	232–245	8–9

Resources

We know that sometimes it feels like you're spending your entire day herding cats (figuratively but also possibly literally if you're really bad at saying no to requests for pets), so to help you save time, we've herded all the best lunch-packing provisions into one place: here. Or go to our store at lunchboxbook.com for a comprehensive and curated selection of our very favorite finds.

BOXES + ACCESSORIES

YUMBOX
yumboxlunch.com
Given its bright palette, whimsical themed inserts, and perfect portioning, don't be surprised if you end up owning one (or three) in every color of the rainbow.

LUNCHBOT
lunchbots.com
Eco-friendly stainless-steel boxes that are deeper and roomier than most, making them a good choice for heartier young eaters and adult snackers alike.

PLANETBOX
planetbox.com
Help Mother Earth and look good doing it. These handsome hinged stainless-steel lunch boxes' smart design and separate lidded dipping containers make portioning easy and fun.

OMIEBOX
omielife.com
Some like it (i.e., their oatmeal/soup/dumplings) hot, and for those eaters, there's this magical thermal-insulated leakproof lunchbox that lets you co-pack warm and cold foods.

BENTGO
bentgo.com
Super-sturdy no-nonsense boxes in your choice of plastic or stainless steel, both reliably leakproof, plus a revolutionizing "chill" design with a built-in ice pack.

CHEREE BERRY PAPER & DESIGN
chereeberrypaperdesign.com
The custom stationery savant happens to also be the bee's knees in lunchbox notes, valentines, teacher notes, and "First Day of School" flags.

HYDROFLASK
hydroflask.com
Even the littlest sippers can manage to open their flip-straw water bottles, which are easy to clean and now easy to label (after oh-so-many lost water bottles, they added a spot for your kid's name on the bottom).

MAISONETTE
maisonette.com
Curated kids' supplies, including a broad selection of lunch bags and backpacks for days when you have hours to fall down the browsing rabbit hole.

NAME BUBBLES
namebubbles.com
Personalized supplies to meet *all* your labeling needs, but, for our purposes, waterproof lunchbox labels that can withstand 7,452 runs in the dishwasher and counting.

SKIPHOP

skiphop.com

Your first stop on the school bus has toddler-size backpacks, insulated lunch bags, and coordinating accessories. (Tip: Label it all; they're very popular.)

ZOKU

zokuhome.com

Utensil sets in designs so darling, your luncher might actually use them.

TOOLS

AMAZON

amazon.com

Any and all lunchbox accessorizing tools can be found here—rice molds and bento picks to add amusement, cute wooden picks for spearing meatballs and melon balls, a set of miniature cookie cutter letters to punch notes out of cheese or etch them into cookies, as well as any number of lunchbox-ready slim ice packs.

ANN CLARK COOKIE CUTTERS

annclarkcookiecutters.com

America's beloved cookie cutter manufacturer makes over 2,400 shapes, from sea turtles and squirrels to snow globes and shamrocks (regular *and* miniature).

LUNCH PUNCH

thelunchpunch.com

Never settle for an ordinary square sandwich again— these sturdy stampers take this midday mainstay to the stars (literally—see the rocket stamp on page 23).

MERI MERI

merimeri.com

Themed napkins, cookie cutters, and picks to supply your party of one.

TARGET

target.com

Gather stickers and stationery for love notes, speed-shop snacks, pick up wee party favors for a small lunchbox compartment, and consider yourself quite restrained and practical if you leave with just one shopping bag.

WILTON CANDY EYEBALLS

wilton.com

Because there are very few lunch items that don't look better with candy eyeballs.

SNACKS

TRADER JOE'S

traderjoes.com

We love TJ's and their bottomless bounty of snacks so much, we penned an ode to it: *Your logo is red / without you, we're blue / O Trader Joe's / how we love you.*

THRIVE

thrivemarket.com

Whatever your little luncher can or can't eat, this exceptionally well-stocked online organic market has it.

INDEX

Marnie Hanel and **Jen Stevenson** are the authors of *The Snowy Cabin Cookbook, Summer: A Cookbook, The Campout Cookbook,* and *The Picnic,* winner of the 2016 IACP Award for Best General Cookbook. Hanel is a journalist who has written about the wild, wonderful ways we live for *The New York Times Magazine, Food & Wine,* and *Vanity Fair.* Stevenson is the author of *Portland's 100 Best Places to Stuff Your Faces* and *Portland Family Adventures.* They both live in Portland, Oregon.